Doctors estimate that nearly 100 million Americans could benefit from a reduction in their blood cholesterol levels. Nutrition and medical experts agree that the easiest way to sharply decrease the serious health risks associated with high levels of cholesterol is by eating oat bran. The innovative and health-conscious recipes found in this book are a wonderfully delicious, sensible way to improve your life and body.

"Oat bran can lower blood-cholesterol levels, thus reducing the risk of high blood pressure and heart attack."

Family Circle

"Health-conscious consumers are rushing out to buy oatmeal, oat bran and oat muffins."

Newsweek

"The word is out that eating oats can lower cholesterol levels in the blood. Result: groceries and supermarkets can't keep oat products on the shelves."

Time

THE OAT BRAN COOKBOOK

Linda Romanelli Leahy

Introduction by Lisa Chobanian, R.N., R.D.

FAWCETT GOLD MEDAL • NEW YORK

Before making any major change in your diet, you should consult your physician.

A Fawcett Gold Medal Book
Published by Ballantine Books
Copyright © 1989 by Lynn Sonberg Book Services

Library of Congress Catalog Card Number: 89-91222

ISBN 0-449-14631-6

This edition published by arrangement with Lynn Sonberg Book Services, 166 East 56th Street, #3C, New York, New York 10022

Manufactured in the United States of America

First Edition: September 1989

Contents

Acknowledgments

Many thanks to Robin Gardiner Zinberg for her help in researching, testing, and editing these recipes—and for lots of laughs while doing it!

Preface

Coronary artery disease remains the leading cause of death in the United States today. While considerable progress has been made in recent years, almost half of all deaths are still due to cardiovascular disease.

Much attention has been given to the prevention of heart disease through controlling one of the major risk factors: elevated blood cholesterol levels. And one of the best ways to control cholesterol levels is through dietary modification.

While the major focus of dietary concern has been on avoidance of saturated fat and cholesterol, recent evidence indicates that eating soluble fiber also helps to control blood cholesterol levels. Since oat bran is an excellent source of soluble fiber, a great deal of concentration has been given to oat bran. Incorporating oat bran into the diet is one of the positive dietary changes which can help control blood cholesterol levels. This practice may be cumbersome however, due to the large amounts needed to be consumed. *The Oat Bran Cookbook* makes consumption of oat bran both easy and enjoyable. The book also provides a comprehensive source of information on oat bran as well as nutrient analysis of each recipe.

By making positive life-style changes that include following a diet low in both total and saturated fat and adding oat bran to your diet, you're on your way to a healthier heart.

Lisa Chobanian, R.N., R.D.

Introduction

WHY ALL THE FUSS ABOUT OAT BRAN?

Oat bran is the brightest star on the nutritional horizon. Newspaper headlines, magazine articles, and respected medical journals all proclaim the good news: oat bran can help to lower cholesterol levels in your blood.

Most of us have gotten the message. The demand for oat bran and oat bran products has soared, far exceeding supply. Supermarkets and health food stores can't keep enough oat bran on their shelves, an array of new oat cereals has been launched by food companies, and long lines form outside of bakeries selling oat bran muffins. Clearly the scientific findings concerning the benefits of oat bran have already had an impact on the way we shop and eat.

It is really little wonder that we all want the peace of mind that a low cholesterol count brings. Heart disease is the leading cause of death in the country, and the amount of cholesterol in your blood is the single most reliable predictor of whether you will fall victim to a heart attack.

The strength of the link between cholesterol and heart disease is really quite dramatic. According to the 1987 report of the National Heart, Lung, and Blood Institute, a 1 percent drop in your blood cholesterol levels means a 2 percent drop in your risk of developing heart disease. If you lower your cholesterol count by 10 percent, your risk of heart disease plummets a full 20 percent!

While it has been known for some time that cholesterol levels can be lowered by the right diet, only recently have health authorities given so much attention to the potential benefits of a single food. In fact, the *Journal for the American Medical Association* has stated that oat bran appears to be the least expensive, least invasive way to reduce cholesterol today!

In short, oat bran seems to be the easy, accessible solution. Is there a hitch?

The hitch is that to get the full cholesterol-lowering benefits of oat bran, you have to eat a lot of it—a cup (uncooked) a day—and you have to eat it regularly day after day. If you relish the thought of eating three bowls of cooked oat bran daily, or if you are prepared to eat six or more oat bran muffins a day (and won't gain weight on them!), and you can tolerate eating this way all of the time, then you may not need this book. If, on the other hand, you are like most people, you need to find appetizing ways to add a cup of oat bran per day to a reasonably heart-healthy diet.

The delicious recipes included in *The Oat Bran Cookbook* will prove that oat bran doesn't have to be boring, but can actually be a delicious adjunct to a healthy diet. Using the Menu Plans (p. 20–23) as well as the oat bran gram counts given for each recipe, you will find it easy to make sure that you are getting the optimum amount of cholesterol-lowering oat bran every day while you still eat appealing, great-tasting, soul-warming food. From soup to dessert, from breakfast foods to midnight snacks, this book shows you delicious easy ways to put oat bran into almost every bite you take. And because the recipes also have been analyzed for calories, saturated fat, cholesterol, sodium, and dietary fiber, you have all the information you need to make oat bran an integral part of a heart-healthy diet.

HOW MUCH OAT BRAN?

In his pioneering studies concerning the favorable impact of oat bran on cholesterol levels in your blood (serum cholesterol), Dr. James Anderson at the University of Kentucky found that people with high cholesterol levels who went on a heart-healthy diet including 100 grams of oat bran daily lowered their cholesterol levels by 21 percent in 21 days. Over two years, the result was a lowering of cholesterol by 25 percent.

He also found that low density lipoprotein (LDL)—the type of cholesterol most strongly linked to heart disease that deposits its waxy, fat-like substance along artery walls—dropped much more substantially in the study subjects than did high density lipoprotein (HDL), the "good" cholesterol that removes cholesterol from the tissues. Dr. Anderson's findings show that oat bran works selectively in the blood to the benefit of those eating it by reducing LDL almost exclusively while leaving the HDL alone. This is one reason why oat bran is so efficient at improving your cholesterol profile.

In addition to consuming 100 grams of oat bran every day, Dr. Anderson's research subjects followed a diet high in complex carbohydrates and dietary fiber, emphasizing whole grains, fresh fruits, and vegetables. Red meat, sugar, and fats were avoided; fish and poultry were eaten for protein.

Dr. Anderson also found in the same study that oat bran helped to stabilize blood sugar, thus playing a helpful role in controlling diabetes. It seems that oat bran slows the absorption of carbohydrates from the stomach. This helps prevent blood sugar from rising after a meal. In his studies, people who suffered from adult-onset diabetes and who went on a high oat bran, high carbohydrate, low-fat diet were able to either stop taking insulin altogether or else were able to substantially reduce the amount they were taking.

Other studies on oat bran have shown similar results. Although the amount of oat bran eaten varies from study to study, the amount needed to lower cholesterol seems to fall within a certain range. Generally good results have been achieved through the daily inclusion of two to three ounces of oat bran (uncooked) daily. This translates into 56 to 84 grams, or about a cup. Once your body has become accustomed to the extra fiber, if you are highly motivated you may want to eat up to 100 grams of oat bran daily for even greater benefits.

It is thought that at least 35 grams of oat bran (about the amount contained in ¾ cup of cooked oat bran) should be eaten daily in order to achieve at least a *minimal* effect on controlling or lowering cholesterol. At 35 grams a day, a 3 percent drop in cholesterol has been noted in two well-constructed studies conducted at Northwestern University Medical School. Of course, for optimal benefits, the recommended daily intake is still from 56 to 84 grams.

Oat Bran Equivalents

Your Goal: Eat 56 to 84 grams of oat bran per day.

1 oz. of dry oat bran
equals about
28 grams dry
equals
1/3 cup dry
equals
2/3 cup cooked

2 oz. of dry oat bran
equals about
56 grams dry
equals
2/3 cup dry
equals
1 1/3 cups cooked

3 oz. of dry oat bran
equals about
84 grams dry
equals
1 cup dry
equals
2 cups cooked

If you faithfully incorporate two to three ounces (56 to 84 grams) of oat bran in a diet that is low in cholesterol and saturated fat, you can expect your serum cholesterol level to drop from 6 to 10 percent within 30 days! If you continue this regimen, it's possible to cut serum cholesterol by as much as 25 percent or even more. Remember, before making any major change in your diet, you should always consult your physician.

HOW OAT BRAN WORKS

We've all heard a great deal about the many benefits of fiber in your diet. Most people equate fiber with wheat bran, the hard outer coating of the grain, but this is only one type of fiber: insoluble fiber. While this type of fiber has many benefits, it will have absolutely no effect on your cholesterol level. Most grains, with the exception of oats, barley, and corn, are rich sources of insoluble fiber.

There is another type of fiber—soluble fiber—that is more gummy or gelatinous than crunchy. This is the active ingredient that makes oat bran an effective tool for lowering serum cholesterol levels. Besides oats and oat bran, rich sources of soluble fiber include dried beans and peas, barley, corn, carrots, and certain fruits and vegetables.

Soluble fiber will literally dissolve in water. Mix a small amount of oat bran with water, and it becomes gummy or sticky. Add water to wheat bran, which contains mostly insoluble fiber, and you will see that the two do not really mix; a layer of what looks like sawdust floats to the surface.

Similarly in the body, insoluble fiber will retain its coarseness and increase bulk in the intestinal tract, where it speeds waste through the system. By speeding up elimination and removing potential carcinogens from the body rapidly, insoluble fiber helps lower the risk of colon cancer. A variety of digestive ailments, including diverticulosis and hemorrhoids, are also less likely to develop on a high-fiber diet.

Soluble fiber, on the other hand, has the demonstrated ability to lower cholesterol levels, although no one understands the mechanism with any precision.

One theory is that soluble fiber binds with bile acids made from cholesterol. These acids aid in the digestion of fat in the intestines. Soluble fiber speeds their movement from the body, removing cholesterol at the same time. There is also evidence that oat bran, after being fermented by bacteria in the large intestine, actually slows down the production of cholesterol in the liver. Another hypothesis holds that soluble fiber coats the intestines, thereby lessening the amount of fat and cholesterol that can be absorbed by the blood. Remember, too, that only the "bad" LDL-type cholesterol is lowered by oat bran, while the "good" HDL-type remains unchanged.

While we may not know exactly how soluble fiber works, the important thing is that it does work—that it does dramatically reduce cholesterol. Remember, that for every one percent drop in cholesterol, you reduce your chances of heart attack by two percent. That two-for-one factor definitely works in your favor! However, keep in mind that cholesterol levels drop the most dramatically in people with the highest counts at the start. Also, oat bran works most effectively when it is accompanied by a heart-healthy diet low in cholesterol and saturated fat.

WHY CHOLESTEROL IS IMPORTANT

Whether or not you develop the most common form of heart disease—hardening of the arteries (atherosclerosis)—depends on a number of factors, but particularly on the amount of excess cholesterol in your blood. It is crucial for everyone, including people with currently low cholesterol levels, to keep serum cholesterol under control in order to avoid heart disease now or in the future.

When there is an excess, or high, level of cholesterol in the blood, cholesterol begins to stick to artery walls, along with cellular debris and other fatty substances. This narrowing can continue until eventually arteries can become completely blocked. When that happens to an artery feeding the heart, the result is a heart attack.

Cholesterol is a product of animal metabolism so it is present in such foods as meat, egg yolk, dairy products, and liver. It also is manufactured by the body for use during metabolism and its presence is vital in building cellular membranes, utilizing vitamins, and producing hormones. When we ingest foods that contain cholesterol, we add to the 1,000 mg or so that the liver and intestines manufacture daily, which is actually more than enough for our daily needs. The amount of cholesterol ingested daily should be no more than 100 mg per 1,000 calories—300 mg, tops.

According to the latest government guidelines, issued in 1987, for individuals 30 years or older, the desirable cholesterol level has been set at under 200 mg per deciliter of blood. Many health authorities, however, feel that this is a liberal level. Widely accepted research shows that the risk of heart disease begins to increase once serum cholesterol levels increase above 150 mg. While clearly the zone of accelerated heart disease risk occurs at levels above 200 mg, these health authorities feel that most adults should aim for a serum cholesterol level below 180 mg. One major study tracking 350,000 men over an eight-year period showed that those with cholesterol levels between 182 and 202 were at substantially higher risk of dying from heart disease than those with cholesterol levels below 180.

The fact is that no one can afford to be careless when it comes to keeping a lid on serum cholesterol counts. The average cholesterol count of 210 mg, while not alarming, should still be a cause for concern. In the past, men have been thought to be at greatest risk for developing high counts, but women's post-menopausal cholesterol levels often catch up with men's, and many even exceed them, so this advantage of being born female is lost at this stage in life. All of us should control cholesterol levels by monitoring them regularly and eating the right foods. Even children should be taught healthy eating habits as a preventive measure, to keep them from developing problems in childhood or later in life.

CHOLESTEROL LOWERING GUIDELINES

No one food—not even oat bran!—can be eaten to the exclusion of all others. Foods work together synergistically. The only way to make sure oat bran will work in your favor is to maintain a balance of nutrients through a low-fat, low-cholesterol diet that also includes substantial amounts of oat bran. You can't expect a cup of oat bran a day to offset an otherwise artery-clogging regimen.

In 1987, the National Cholesterol Education Program convened a panel of experts in association with more than 20 major medical associations. The guidelines issued by this panel regarding healthy eating echo similar suggestions by the American Heart Association, the National Cancer Institute, the National Academy of Sciences National Research Council, and the Surgeon General's "Report on Preventive Medicine" (1980). Similarly, U.S. Government dietary guidelines call for the same things: weight reduction; less cholesterol, saturated, and overall fat intake; and increased consumption of fiber. These august groups also suggested that salt and sugar consumption be cut; that salt-cured, smoked, and pickled foods be limited; and that intake of fish be increased in order to get the Omega-3 fatty acid found in fish and in shellfish. (Omega-3 is also thought to help lower cholesterol.) It was further recommended that a greater amount of protein be obtained from vegetable sources such as legumes and grains as a means to temper the American love affair with red meat.

GUIDELINES FOR HEALTHY LOW-CHOLESTEROL EATING

It makes good sense to keep your daily diet to one of balance and moderation. When setting up a healthful diet, include foods from each of the major food groups:

Dairy (choose low-fat products)
Lean meat, poultry, or fish
Grains and cereals
Fruits and vegetables (including legumes)

Then follow these guidelines:

1. *Limit saturated fats and cholesterol.* Foods to avoid include: Fatty red meats, butter, cheese, eggs, whole milk products, chocolate, lard, coconut oil, palm kernel oil, hydrogenated and partially hydrogenated vegetable oils, fried foods.
2. *Increase protein intake from vegetable sources.* Legumes and soy products such as tofu are high in vegetable protein.
3. *Increase consumption of complex carbohydrates,* dietary fiber, fruits, and vegetables.
4. *Increase consumption of fish and shellfish,* which contain Omega-3 fatty acid, a substance believed to lower cholesterol levels.
5. Limit consumption of salt and refined sugar.

TIPS FOR ADDING FIBER TO YOUR DIET

Even eating 56 to 84 grams of oat bran daily does not mean you will be getting the total dietary—soluble and insoluble—fiber you need for an all-around healthy diet. The National Cancer Institute recommends including 25 to 35 grams of dietary fiber per day in any eating program. One-third cup of dry oat bran provides 4.2 grams of dietary fiber. Eating a cup of oat bran (uncooked) per day, as we recommend, will give you approximately 25 grams total dietary fiber daily. You can get the rest of your day's fiber needs through eating fruits, vegetables, and whole grains. Drink plenty of liquids while eating a fiber-rich diet to help the fiber work best, and add fiber gradually to the diet in order to avoid abdominal discomfort as your body adjusts to your new regimen.

Here are some tips for adding fiber to your diet:

- Eat raw fruits and vegetables with the skins on.
- Eat whole grain breads and cereals.
- Include corn, broccoli, and apples in your menus.
- Eat brown rather than white rice.
- Eat dried beans (don't overcook).
- Add dried beans or peas to soups and stews.
- Snack on raw vegetables.
- Eat fruit instead of drinking fruit juices.

When oat bran is eaten as part of a low-fat, low-cholesterol high-fiber eating program, it can play its part in lowering cholesterol without interference. The recipes in this book are specially designed to help you eat a wholesome, low-fat, low-cholesterol, high oat bran diet. You can eat well and enjoy it, too!

COOKING WITH OATS AND OAT BRAN

The recipes in this book contain one or more of the following oat products: oat bran, oat groats, steel-cut oats, rolled oats, oat flour, oat cereal flakes, and oat sprouts. You probably have rolled oats in your cupboard right now, but you may not be familiar with oat flour, oat groats, or steel-cut oats. This book will help you use oat bran and other oat products in an array of appetizing, healthful recipes that will appeal to everyone interested in good food and good health.

The various oat products available in supermarkets and health food stores vary in their soluble fiber content, and they also require different cooking procedures. Depending on how the oats have been processed, oat products differ in their handling requirements as well as in the taste they impart. Since oats remain basically unrefined—or only lightly refined—throughout their processing stages, they do not lose their important bran and germ, which means they keep most of their nutrients in all forms.

Oats and oat products provide more high quality protein than any other grain. Oats also contain carbohydrates, B-vitamins, vitamin E, and nine minerals. One ounce of oat bran provides just 110 calories, yet oat bran tends to be filling, giving a satiated feeling without heavy intake of food. Since surplus weight is also linked to heart disease, this is another reason to find ways to work oat bran into your meals.

In general, oat products absorb a great deal of liquid during preparation as well as inside the body. This is a result of their high soluble fiber content, which makes them so beneficial. It also means that you may have to get used to using more liquid with oat bran or other oat dishes in order to keep them from getting overly dry.

Of all the oat products, oat bran contains the highest concentration of soluble fiber and vitamins. Most cholesterol-related research has been done using oat bran alone. However, some studies, particularly those conducted at Northwestern University Medical School, studied the relationship between oatmeal and serum cholesterol, perhaps because of oatmeal's high degree of popularity with the consumer. These studies found that oatmeal also has beneficial effects. In these studies, researchers discovered that as little as 35 grams of oat bran *or* oatmeal eaten daily will lower cholesterol by about 3 percent. Another study showed that two ounces of oatmeal (56 gm) brought down cholesterol levels by 9.3 percent when accompanied by a low-fat diet.

Some sources say that whole oat products contain 80 percent of the soluble fiber in oat bran while others give the correct amount as 50 percent. Because different chemical methods for analyzing soluble fiber are used by different researchers, the results obtained are not yet uniform. While it would seem that oatmeal should theoretically have less power to lower cholesterol than oat bran, the results of scientific studies to date do not bear this out. For this reason, we have used the higher 80 percent figure in estimating the oat bran content of the recipes in this book that use whole oat products. Clearly much of the benefits of oat bran can be obtained by eating oatmeal, groats, oat flour, and so on, along with oat bran.

Use the recipes in this book, then branch out and experiment with the many varieties of this enormously healthful grain. On the pages that follow, you'll find everything you need to know about cooking with different oat products.

Oat Bran

This is the bran-only portion of the oat kernel, the hard outer coating of the grain. Of all the oat products it has the highest concentration of nutrients as well as soluble fiber (the soluble fiber lies in the bran). Oat bran is also higher in protein and lower in carbohydrates than other oat products. It comes in a grainy type of flour that can itself be made into a hot cereal, similar to Wheatena. Cooking time is three minutes or less. Flavor cooked oat bran cereal with a sprinkling of brown sugar, a few raisins, or some fresh fruit. Some brands of oat bran are grainier than others, but there is not a significant difference when cooking.

Oat bran swells significantly and absorbs liquid quickly. Be sure to use the correct amount of liquid to obtain best results. Always check the liquid during cooking time and add liquid if necessary.

Oat bran is beneficial raw or cooked. Eating it raw

may sound unappetizing, but oat bran can be sprinkled over the top of puddings or salads. You can thicken salad dressings with a teaspoon or so of oat bran per serving. This adds a pleasant nutty flavor and makes the dressing coat the salad ingredients better. The point is that to get the benefits, oat bran can be eaten any way you please.

Substitute up to half oat bran for your flour in cakes, pastries, cookies, pancakes, and breads. (If you sift it, the bran may sift out, so be sure you put that bran back in to whatever you are baking.) Use oat bran instead of bread crumbs to extend tuna or meat loaf or patties; just be sure to include additional liquid (such as water or tomato sauce), enough to make a workable consistency. Oat bran makes an excellent thickener for soups, but the soup must be served immediately. If reheated, the soup will become gelatinous.

Oat Groats

Oat groats is the name given to the whole oat kernel with only the inedible cover, or husk, removed. The groat contains both the bran and the germ. It is a whole grain oat. Processing turns it into pieces or flakes which are then called something else, but the groat itself can be cooked and eaten as it is. It has a delicately nutty flavor similar to brown rice.

To cook oat groats, use a ratio of two parts water to one part groats. Cover and simmer for about 45 minutes. Add groats to soup or stews about 45 minutes before finishing time. Serve as a side dish instead of rice or potatoes, use to stuff fish or Rock Cornish hens, or make into a main course Middle Eastern-style salad by adding such things as pea pods, red pepper slivers, and water chestnuts, then topping with a light, oil-free dressing. You can grind groats yourself by blending them on the ''grind'' setting of your blender for a minute or so until the texture is fine. Then use ground groats as a thickening or coating instead of bread crumbs.

Steel-Cut Oats

These are made from oat groats that are sliced into two or three pieces. There is little to no heat used in this processing, so these oats retain most of the groat's B vitamins and flavor. They take about 30 minutes to cook into a porridge (definitely Scottish style, thick, possibly lumpy), and they can be used in most recipes that call for whole rolled oats. Add steel-cut oats to pancakes, cookies, and those dense biscuits called scones.

Rolled Oats

These are flakes cut from the groat, which is first flattened and rolled. Heat is used to soften the oats and to make them cook more quickly. The result is that you can cook whole rolled oats into oatmeal in five minutes.

The one-minute—or "quick"—rolled oats are more heavily processed and cook into breakfast cereal in one minute. Because of the heat used in processing, some nutrients are lost.

In both types of rolled oats, bran is included, since they both come from the groat, which contains the bran.

Use rolled oats in cookies, muffins, and a whole variety of ways shown in the recipes that follow, as well as for that all-time breakfast favorite, steamy hot cereal served with skim milk.

Instant oats are not recommended because heavy processing destroys too many nutrients as well as too much soluble fiber. Most instant oats also come with sugar and salt added.

Oat Flour

Usually health food stores carry oat flour already milled. If you buy prepackaged oat flour, make sure by reading the label that the bran has been retained. Or, make your own flour from groats, steel-cut oats, or whole oats. Blend at a high speed for about one minute until the oats reach a sifting consistency. Stir up from the bottom from time to time as you blend. When grinding whole rolled oats, you'll find that you "lose" about 1/4 cup in the process, so to get one cup of flour, blend one and a quarter cups of oatmeal. Your flour will be as nutritious and effective as the oat product you use to make it.

Use oat flour for baking. In breads, it adds flavor, but because oat flour lacks the gluten that makes bread rise, the dough must be heavily kneaded. Recipes that do not call for yeast, such as muffins and pancakes, can easily absorb oat flour as at least one-third of the total flour called for. When substituting oat flour for whole wheat flour, use half again as much oat flour. (For example, if the recipe calls for one cup of whole wheat flour, use one and a half cups of oat flour.)

You'll find many other ways to use oat flour. Use it to "bread" fish or chicken; it will seal in juices and add a pleasant, nutty flavor. You can also thicken cereals, puddings, and sauces with oat flour. Store oat flour as you would any flour, in a container with a tight-fitting lid.

Ready-to-Eat Oat Cereals
Many cereals now come either with oat bran added or with oats as a main ingredient. It's hard to know just how much oat bran you will get with these, since the labels don't tell you. Read ingredient labels carefully and note the order in which oats appear. If oats are not listed as the first ingredient, the product probably does not contain a substantial amount. You can also try calling the manufacturer for information. Avoid any products processed with saturated fats such as coconut oil, since adding fat to oats is counterproductive.

The bottom line is, while ready-to-eat cereals can certainly contribute oat bran to your diet, most nationally distributed brands do not contain enough bran for you to rely on them as a mainstay. According to a report in *Nutrition Action*, a newsletter published by The Center for Science in the Public Interest, as of this writing, only four national brands contain eight or more grams of oat bran per serving. In comparison, cooked oat bran cereal contains 28 grams of oat bran per ⅔ cup serving. The brands are:

	SERVING	OAT BRAN (g)
Kellogg's Common Sense Oat Bran	⅔ cup	13.0
Kellogg's Cracklin' Oat Bran	½ cup	9.0
New Morning Oatios with Oat Bran	1 cup	8.4
General Mills Cheerios	1¼ cups	8.0

NOTE: Kölln Oat Bran Crunch, imported from West Germany, is extremely high in oat bran at 20 grams per serving, but it is expensive and may not be available in your area. Check with your local health food store if you wish to sample this cereal.

Cooking tip: You can make delicious crumbs from cereal flakes by placing the flakes in a sealable plastic bag and crushing them with a rolling pin.

Oat Sprouts

Sprouts are another good way to get your daily oats. They're rich in nutrients—like most sprouts—and also high in vitamin C. To grow oat sprouts, buy them whole, untreated, and still in their hulls. Prepare them as you would any sprout; rinse them first, then soak them overnight. Then rinse and drain them daily for the next two to four days. Keep the growing oat sprouts in a jar with a perforated top or fasten a cheesecloth over the top with a rubber band. It's important that air circulate inside the jar. When the sprouts are about double their initial length, store them in the refrigerator. Include sprouts in salads, pita sandwiches, breads, and even stews.

Storing Oats

Oats contain a natural preservative, so they will keep longer than most grains. However, it's still a good idea to store your oats in an air-tight container in the refrigerator for longer life.

Toasting Oats

Toasted oats are an easy way to add oats to your everyday meals. They can be sprinkled on top of puddings or desserts along with fruit and nuts, stirred into yogurt, or used as a topping for fruit cobblers and crisps. Top vegetable dishes or casseroles with toasted oats for a crunchy crust. Wherever you would use nuts, even for snacking, think instead of toasted oats. Add toasted oats to ready-to-eat cereal to bolster its bran content.

You can make your own toasted oats by spreading rolled oats or oat groats lightly on a cookie sheet. Place in a 350° F. oven for 15 minutes, stirring occasionally. Or, toast oats in a dry skillet over medium heat. Even oat bran can be toasted, but will require less cooking time.

Making Substitutions

It's easy to be creative with oats, and you'll find many new ways to use oats in various forms. When using the recipes that follow, it's important to use the specific oat product that is listed, since substitutions may affect the finished product. An exception: old-fashioned rolled oats, quick rolled oats, and steel-cut oats are interchangeable.

Safflower or sunflower oil are the healthiest choices

when "vegetable oil" is listed as an ingredient. Fats should be used as written. In baked goods, tub margarine will react slightly differently from stick margarine, and texture may be sacrificed.

Freezing Baked Goods

Baked goods lose moisture rapidly, so it's a good idea to wrap your oat goodies tightly and freeze them. You can easily reheat frozen muffins in the microwave (it takes about 40 seconds, depending upon the size of the muffin) or in the conventional oven (wrap the frozen muffin in foil and heat it in a preheated 350° F. oven for about 15 minutes).

While the vast majority of recipes in this book are extremely healthful—low in fat and cholesterol, high in fiber, and low to moderate in sodium—they do not necessarily conform to strict dietary guidelines. For example, a few recipes use cheese, we've included a great recipe for stuffed pork chops, and a number of desserts are definitely for special occasions only. If you are on a special diet, be sure to read the nutrition analyses given with each recipe for information on calories, cholesterol, saturated fat, sodium, dietary fiber, and of course, oat bran.

USING THE MENU PLANS

It has been shown that eating oat bran throughout the day rather than consuming your daily quota all at one sitting (hard as this is to imagine) is the most effective way of lowering cholesterol counts. The menu plan that follows shows how to incorporate the oat bran recipes in this book into an effective cholesterol-lowering eating plan that can be carried on through three meals and into snacks. It is moderate in calories, providing approximately 2000 per day. You may wish to follow the meal plan exactly or else use it as a guide for constructing your own menus.

Sample Menu Plan*
Calories per day: about 2000

DAY	BREAKFAST	LUNCH
MON 1	*Strawberry-Banana Perk-Up* *Hot Groats and Honey* Decaf coffee	*High-Fiber Burger and Sprouts with Puffed ''Pita'' Sandwich Roll* Sliced avocado* and tomatoes Diet soda *use sparingly
TUES 2	Stewed prunes *Anise—Scented Egg Puff* Decaf espresso Skim milk, 1 glass	*Sausage Stuffed Tomato* Cucumber Salad Lime-flavored seltzer
WED 3	Cantaloupe *Cashew—Apricot Granola* *Chocolate Tofu Shake*	*Smoked Chicken Salad on Wild Greens with Balsamic Vinaigrette* French bread Natural spring water
THURS 4	Chilled Applesauce *Cinnamon Pumpkin Pancakes* Skim milk, 1 glass	Lowfat cottage cheese with lemon pepper and oat sprouts on Romaine *Garden Vegetable Muffin* Iced herbal tea
FRI 5	½ grapefruit *Hi-Power Oat Bran Muffin* Decaf coffee Skim milk, 1 glass	*Basil-Oat ''Fritters'' with Tri-Color Peppers* Sliced part-skim mozzarella and olives Iced cappuccino
SAT 6	Mimosa* (o.j. and champagne) *Black Walnut Waffles with Raspberry-Mint Coulis* Decaf coffee	*Warm Lentils with Lemon Vinaigrette* *Jumbo Onion-Dill Popover* Diet soda

DINNER	SNACK	TOTAL OAT BRAN (g)
Parmesan-Black Olive Bread *Pasta with Chick Peas and Spinach Pesto* Tomato and onion vinaigrette Chianti, 1 glass	Mixed vegetable juice Rice cake, 1 Non-fat yogurt, 1 cup	66
Crunchy Baked Chicken *Corn Creole* Steamed broccoli *Gingered Pear Cobbler* Iced tea	*Tiny Tofu Teacakes* (3) Skim milk, 1 glass	75
South of the Border Pizza Succotash *Crunchy Oatmeal Cookies* (2) Peach nectar spritzer	Sliced strawberries, ½ cup Non-fat yogurt, 1 cup	72
Chili Pot Pie with Pepper Crust Mixed green salad with asparagus tips *Apple Crisp* Lemon-flavored seltzer	*Carrot Cake* Skim milk, 1 glass	61
Turkey Meatloaf *Metro Macaroni and Cheese* Mushroom and spinach salad Skim milk, 1 glass	*Caramel Popcorn Balls* (2)	71
Spinach Soup with Herb Dumplings *Baked Snapper with Julienne of Vegetables* *Raisin-Bread Pudding* Chardonnay, 1 glass	*Ice Milk Malted*	80

DAY	BREAKFAST	LUNCH
SUN 7	Orange-Pineapple Juice *Oat Crepes with Bananas and "Sour Cream"* Skim milk, 1 glass	*Grilled Quail with Brandied Sweet Potato Croquettes* Orange and red onions with balsamic vinegar Seltzer

DINNER	SNACK	TOTAL OAT BRAN (g)
Spicy Cocktail Scallops Wontons in Soy-Ginger Sauce Stir-fry vegetables Tropical Fruit Plate (pineapple, kiwi, papaya, carambola) Light beer, 1 glass	*Burnt Almond Gelato*	79

With oat bran (OB) gram counts provided for each recipe, your calculations for the day will be simple. You'll know if you need that midnight granola/oat snack or whether you've gotten in your grams for the day without it. The recipes have also been analyzed for calories, cholesterol, saturated fat, total fat, sodium, and dietary fiber. Whether you need a special diet or not, your health and that of your entire family will benefit from oat bran in these delicious, healthful recipes.

If you have been consuming a low-fiber diet until now, do not attempt your full quota of oat bran immediately. Begin gradually, then work up to your goal of 56 to 84 grams a day. Once your system has become accustomed to this amount, for even greater benefits, you may safely consume up to 100 grams of oat bran daily.

Lisa Chobanian, R.N., R.D.

THE RECIPES

Appetizers

Tuna Toppers

Makes 4 servings.

These fish balls make a great first course with a crisp white wine, or serve them as an hors d'oeuvre with cocktails.

Oat Bran (g): 16	
Calories: 188	Total Fat (g): 9
Cholesterol (mg): 17	Sodium (mg): 408
Sat. Fat (g): 1	Fiber (g): 2
All counts are per serving	

3/4 *cup oat bran*	2 *tablespoons chopped*
3/4 *cup chicken broth*	*fresh parsley*
1/4 *cup dry white wine*	1 *small shallot, minced*
One 6½-ounce can light	1/4 *teaspoon cayenne*
meat tuna, packed in	*pepper*
water, drained and	2 *tablespoons olive oil*
flaked	
1 *large egg white*	

1. In medium bowl, combine ½ cup of the oat bran with 3 tablespoons of the chicken broth and 1 tablespoon of the wine.

2. Add tuna, egg white, parsley, shallot, cayenne pepper; mix well.
3. Form mixture into 1½-inch balls.
4. Place remaining oat bran on wax paper; roll tuna balls in oat bran to coat.
5. In 12-inch nonstick skillet, heat oil over medium heat; brown tuna balls on all sides.
6. Add the remaining broth and wine; reduce heat, cover, and cook 30 minutes, adding more broth if necessary.

Sesame Cheese Log

Makes 8 servings.

This log gets better after a day or two in the refrigerator. Since this recipe is fairly high in saturated fat, you may want to reserve it for special occasions.

Oat Bran (g): 8	
Calories: 206	Total Fat (g): 19
Cholesterol (mg): 7	Sodium (mg): 334
Sat. Fat (g): 5	Fiber (g): 2
All counts are per serving	

³/₄   cup oat bran
¹/₄   cup sesame seeds
¹/₂   teaspoon paprika
One 8-ounce tub reduced-fat cream cheese at room temperature
¹/₂ cup crumbled blue cheese (about 2¹/₂ ounces)
¹/₄ cup imitation sour cream
1   small onion, finely chopped

1. To toast oat bran and sesame seeds, spray a 12-inch nonstick skillet with nonstick cooking spray; add bran and seeds and toast over medium heat 3 to 4 minutes or until lightly browned, stirring frequently. Remove from heat and stir in paprika. Reserve 1/4 cup of this mixture.

2. In medium bowl, combine cheeses, sour cream, onion, and the remaining bran/sesame seed mixture; refrigerate, covered, until firm, about 2 hours.

3. On a 16-inch length of wax paper, spoon cheese mixture into a 9-inch strip lengthwise down center of paper. Fold wax paper in half over cheese strip, pressing in to form cylinder. With a ruler, push in toward cylinder to form a firm, tight roll about 1 1/2 inches wide and 10 inches long.

4. Place reserved oat bran mixture on another sheet of wax paper; roll log in mixture, turning to coat. Press any remaining mixture into log and roll up in wax paper, turning ends under to close.

5. Refrigerate overnight for blending of flavors.

Spicy Cocktail Scallops

Makes 4 servings.

Sea scallops, the larger scallop with a delicate briny flavor, is perfect hors d'oeuvre fare. Serve these hot from the oven, with lemon wedges.

Oat Bran (g): 8

Calories: 157   Total Fat (g): 4
Cholesterol (mg): 37   Sodium (mg): 337
Sat. Fat (g): < 1   Fiber (g): 1

All counts are per serving

---

6 tablespoons oat bran   1 pound sea scallops
1 teaspoon chili powder   1 large egg white, lightly
1/4 teaspoon salt   beaten
                              2 teaspoons vegetable oil

1. Preheat oven to 425° F.; spray a baking sheet with nonstick cooking spray; set aside.
2. In a medium bowl, combine oat bran, chili powder, and salt. Dip scallops in egg white; dredge in oat bran mixture to coat.
3. Place scallops on prepared pan; drizzle with oil.
4. Bake 8 to 10 minutes, until scallops are cooked.

Cheesy Pecan Shortbread
Makes 28 shortbread rounds.

This is a "cocktail" shortbread. These rounds are even better with hickory-smoked pecans, if you can track them down.

Oat Bran (g): 3

Calories: 74   Total Fat (g): 5
Cholesterol (mg): 4   Sodium (mg): 83
Sat. Fat (g): 1   Fiber (g): < 1

All counts are per serving of two rounds

½ cup margarine at room temperature	*½ cup oat bran*
One 4-ounce package shredded Cheddar cheese* (1 cup)	*¼ teaspoon each cayenne pepper and salt*
1 cup all-purpose flour	*28 pecan halves*

1. Preheat oven to 325° F.
2. In large bowl, cream the margarine; add cheese, flour, oat bran, pepper and salt, mix with fork, then combine dough with hands.
3. Roll dough into 1-inch balls; place on ungreased baking sheet. Moisten bottom of a glass and press down on each ball to flatten. Press in pecan halves.
4. Bake 20 minutes; remove to wire rack to cool.

*1 cup reduced-fat Cheddar-flavored cheese may be used, although the texture won't be as flaky.

Breakfast Foods

Hi-Power Oat Bran Muffin
Makes 8 muffins.

A great muffin to start the day, flavored with nutmeg, honey, and raisins.

Oat Bran (g): 9

Calories: 209   Total Fat (g): 4
Cholesterol (mg): < 1   Sodium (mg): 352
Sat. Fat (g): < 1   Fiber (g): 3

All counts are per serving

1½ cups Kellogg's
   Common Sense Oat
   Bran
¾ cup all-purpose flour
¾ cup oat bran
2 teaspoons baking
   powder
¾ teaspoon ground
   nutmeg

¼ teaspoon salt
½ cup raisins
½ cup egg substitute
¼ cup honey
½ cup skim milk
¼ cup reduced-calorie tub
   margarine, melted and
   cooled

1. Preheat oven to 400° F.; spray eight 2¾-inch muffin cups with nonstick cooking spray; set aside.
2. In sealable plastic bag, crush Kellogg's Oat Bran with a rolling pin into fine crumbs.
3. In medium bowl, stir together oat crumbs, flour, oat bran, baking powder, nutmeg, and salt; add raisins and stir to combine.
4. In small bowl, mix together egg substitute, milk, honey, and margarine. Add to dry ingredients, mixing with fork until just combined; do not overmix.
5. Divide batter evenly among prepared cups.
6. Bake 20–25 minutes, or until toothpick inserted in center comes out clean.
7. Remove muffins from pan; place on rack to cool.

Cinnamon Pumpkin Pancakes

Makes 8 pancakes or 4 servings.

These are thick and scrumptious. No one will remain in bed when the aroma of fresh pancakes wafts through the house.

Oat Bran (g): 10

Calories: 314	Total Fat (g): 9
Cholesterol (mg): 2	Sodium (mg): 403
Sat. Fat (g): 1	Fiber (g): 4

All counts are per serving

1¼ cups skim milk

½ cup canned pumpkin purée

2 tablespoons vegetable oil

1 large egg white, lightly beaten

1 teaspoon vanilla extract

1 cup all-purpose flour

½ cup oat bran

1 tablespoon granulated sugar

2 teaspoons baking powder

¼ teaspoon salt

¾ teaspoon ground cinnamon

½ cup rolled oats

1. In medium bowl, combine milk, pumpkin, 1 tablespoon of the oil, egg white, and vanilla.
2. In separate bowl, combine all the dry ingredients, then add to milk mixture, stirring until just blended. Cover with plastic wrap; let stand 5 minutes.
3. Brush 12-inch nonstick skillet or pancake griddle with remaining oil; heat to medium high.
4. Pour heaping ¼ cup batter on griddle; spread with a spoon to make one 4-inch pancake. (The batter is thick.)
5. Cook 2 to 3 minutes on each side, or until golden; repeat using all the batter.
6. Serve with syrup, jam, or confectioners' sugar.

Hot Groats and Honey

Makes 4 servings.

Beware, this breakfast may evoke images of a blustery day in Scotland. It'll warm you to your toes.

Oat Bran (g): 17

Calories: 111   Total Fat (g): 1
Cholesterol (mg): 0   Sodium (mg): 93
Sat. Fat (g): 0   Fiber (g): 3

All counts are per serving

---

1 cup oat groats, rinsed   *1 tablespoon honey*
and drained   *¹/4 teaspoon ground*
1 ripe Bartlett pear,   *cinnamon*
pared, cored and
chopped

1. In medium saucepan, over high heat, bring 2 cups of water to a boil; stir in groats; cover, reduce heat, and simmer about 45 minutes, or until water is absorbed.
2. Remove from heat; stir in remaining ingredients and serve.

Anise-Scented Egg Puff

Makes 4 servings.

This is an easy yet elegant do-ahead dish that you'll want to serve weekend guests. The anise flavor adds unexpected zip.

Oat Bran (g): 19	
Calories: 311	Total Fat (g): 3
Cholesterol (mg): 4	Sodium (mg): 388
Sat. Fat (g): < 1	Fiber (g): 3.5

All counts are per serving

1¼ cups *evaporated skim milk*
1 cup *egg substitute*
½ cup *oat bran*
½ cup *rolled oats*
2 tablespoons *granulated sugar*
1 teaspoon *vanilla extract*
1 teaspoon *grated orange peel*
½ teaspoon *crushed anise seeds or extract*
6 slices *firm-textured white bread, cut in half on diagonal*
Confectioners' sugar to garnish, optional

1. Spray 7 x 11-inch baking dish with nonstick cooking spray.
2. In medium bowl, whisk together all ingredients except bread.
3. Place bread slices in prepared dish in 2 rows, side by side, overlapping; pour milk mixture evenly over bread. Cover with plastic wrap and refrigerate overnight.
4. The next day, preheat oven to 350° F.; bake about 30 minutes, or until lightly browned and puffed.
5. Sprinkle with confectioners' sugar, if desired, and serve immediately.

Cashew-Apricot Granola

Makes 6 cups (12 servings).

Granola is not just a breakfast food. This deliciously crunchy mixture will jazz up plain nonfat yogurt, ice milk, even cold soups without cereal box sweetness.

Oat Bran (g): 20

Calories: 222	Total Fat (g): 8
Cholesterol (mg): 0	Sodium (mg): 48
Sat. Fat (g): 1	Fiber (g): 4

All counts are per serving

---

3 cups rolled oats
1/2 cup oat bran
1/2 cup wheat germ
1/2 cup raw cashews, chopped
1/4 cup sesame seeds

1/4 teaspoon salt
1/3 cup honey
2 tablespoons vegetable oil
1 teaspoon vanilla extract
1/2 cup chopped dried apricots

1. Preheat oven to 300° F.; spray a jelly-roll pan with nonstick cooking spray; set aside.
2. In large bowl, combine rolled oats, oat bran, wheat germ, cashews, sesame seeds, and salt.
3. In 2-cup measure, combine honey, oil, and vanilla with 1/2 cup water; pour over oat mixture and stir until mixture is crumbly.
4. Spread mixture onto prepared pan; bake 50 to 60 minutes until lightly browned, stirring every 15 minutes.
5. Cool completely, then stir in apricots. Store in airtight container.

Black Walnut Waffles with Raspberry-Mint Coulis

Makes 7 servings of 2 waffles.

The distinct nutty flavor of black walnuts takes a standard waffle to new heights. The raspberry coulis will add an unexpected, elegant touch.

Oat Bran (g): 12

Calories: 298   Total Fat (g): 13
Cholesterol (mg): 40   Sodium (mg): 345
Sat. Fat (g): 1   Fiber (g): 3.5

All counts are per serving

Coulis:

1   tablespoon packed fresh mint leaves
1½ cups fresh or frozen (thawed) whole raspberries

3   tablespoons granulated sugar
1   teaspoon vanilla extract
1–2 tablespoons orange-flavored liqueur, optional

Batter:

1   cup all-purpose flour
1   cup oat bran
2   tablespoons granulated sugar
2½ teaspoons baking powder
½   teaspoon baking soda
¼   teaspoon salt

1¾ cups skim milk
¼   cup vegetable oil
1   large egg plus 2 large egg whites
1   teaspoon vanilla extract
¼   cup finely chopped black walnuts*

---

*Available in specialty food stores. Otherwise, use regular walnuts.

1. To prepare coulis, in food processor fitted with steel blade, chop mint; add remaining ingredients and purée. Place in small saucepan, over medium heat; bring mixture to a boil. Remove from heat; cover and keep warm.
2. To prepare batter, in large bowl, combine dry ingredients. In medium bowl, combine milk, oil, egg and whites, and vanilla. Add to dry ingredients, mixing well. Fold in nuts.
3. Preheat waffle iron.
4. Cook waffles according to your waffle iron manufacturer's instructions.

Basic Oat Pancakes
Makes twelve 4-inch pancakes or 4 servings.

These are wonderfully light pancakes, a perfect base for the addition of your favorite nuts or fruit.

Oat Bran (g): 17

Calories: 188	Total Fat (g): 6
Cholesterol (mg): 70	Sodium (mg): 452
Sat. Fat (g): 1	Fiber (g): 2.5

All counts are per serving

---

1 cup oat flour	1/4 teaspoon salt
1 1/2 tablespoons granulated sugar	1 cup skim milk
2 1/2 teaspoons baking powder	1 large egg, lightly beaten
	1 tablespoon vegetable oil

1. In medium bowl, sift together dry ingredients.
2. In 2-cup measure, combine milk, egg, and oil; add to dry ingredients, mixing well.
3. In 12-inch nonstick skillet or griddle sprayed with nonstick cooking spray, over medium-high heat, pour 2 tablespoons of the batter for each pancake. Cook until cakes are bubbly on top and undersides are lightly browned. Turn with spatula and brown other side. Place cooked pancakes on plate; cover with foil to keep warm.
4. Repeat using all the batter, removing skillet from heat to spray with nonstick cooking spray after each batch of pancakes is made.

Oat Crepes with Bananas and "Sour Cream"

Makes 8 crepes or 4 servings.
This brunch dish tastes positively sinful but is actually quite moderate in calories.

Oat Bran (g): 19

Calories: 322	Total Fat (g): 8
Cholesterol (mg): 3	Sodium (mg): 209
Sat. Fat (g): 6	Fiber (g): 4

All counts are per serving

Filling:
1/2 cup rolled oats
1/2 cup imitation sour cream
1/2 cup plain lowfat yogurt

2 tablespoons confectioners' sugar
1/2 teaspoon almond extract
3 bananas, sliced

Crepe:

1 cup skim milk
1/2 cup egg substitute
1/2 cup oat bran
1/4 cup all-purpose flour
1 tablespoon confectioners' sugar

1/2 teaspoon baking powder
Pinch of salt
Confectioners' sugar to garnish, optional

1. To prepare filling, in small skillet, over medium heat, toast rolled oats 5 to 7 minutes until lightly browned, stirring frequently.
2. In medium bowl, combine all filling ingredients except bananas; stir in bananas; set aside.
3. To prepare crepe, in blender, combine milk and egg substitute; process to blend.
4. Add oat bran, flour, sugar, baking powder, and salt; process until smooth.
5. Spray a crepe pan or 8-inch nonstick sauté pan with nonstick cooking spray. Heat over medium-high heat until a drop of water jumps across pan.
6. For each crepe, pour 1/4 cup of the batter into center of pan; immediately rotate pan until batter covers bottom. Cook 1 to 2 minutes, until underside is light brown and dry; run spatula around edges and lift out. Turn and cook 1 minute longer. Place crepe on foil.
7. After each crepe is lifted from pan, remove pan from heat and spray with nonstick cooking spray. Repeat with remaining batter, making eight 6-inch crepes.
8. Fill each crepe with 1/3 cup of the filling. Sprinkle with confectioners' sugar, if desired.

= Salads and Light Meals =

High-Fiber Burger and Sprouts
Makes 4 servings.

Serve on "puffed" pita sandwich (p. 102). In addition to sprouts, add shredded lettuce, tomato, and onion.

Oat Bran (g): 16 (with pita)

Calories: 590	Total Fat (g): 28
Cholesterol (mg): 123	Sodium (mg): 367
Sat. Fat (g): 8	Fiber (g): 5.5

All counts are per serving

½ cup Kellogg's Common Sense Oat Bran
1¼ pounds lean ground beef
2 tablespoons oat bran
¼ cup egg substitute
2 teaspoons Worcestershire sauce
2 teaspoons spicy brown mustard
½ cup sprouts
4 "puffed" pita sandwich rolls
Low-sodium ketchup, optional

1. Preheat broiler.
2. In sealable plastic bag, crush Kellogg's Oat Bran with rolling pin into fine crumbs.

3. In large bowl, combine all ingredients except ketchup; work lightly with fingers to combine.
4. Shape into 4 patties (about 1 inch thick). Broil on rack, 4 inches from heat, 5 minutes on each side, for medium doneness.
5. Place each burger inside a puffed pita; top with equal amounts of sprouts and ketchup, if desired.

Sausage Stuffed Tomatoes
Makes 4 servings.

A surprise burst of fennel flavor adds excitement to this luncheon dish.

Oat Bran (g): 16

Calories: 268	Total Fat (g): 17
Cholesterol (mg): 22	Sodium (mg): 500
Sat. Fat (g): 4	Fiber (g): 5.5

All counts are per serving

---

4 *large beefsteak tomatoes*	1/4 *teaspoon fennel seeds*
1/2 *teaspoon salt*	1/4 *teaspoon red pepper flakes*
2 *tablespoons olive oil*	1/4 *pound sweet Italian sausage*
1 *small onion, finely chopped*	3/4 *cup oat bran*
1 *garlic clove, minced*	2 *cups Bibb lettuce to garnish, optional*

1. Preheat oven to 350° F.; spray an 8-inch square baking dish with nonstick cooking spray; set aside.
2. Wash and dry tomatoes. Cut off tops with a serrated knife; scoop out pulp, leaving shell; reserve pulp.
3. Sprinkle inside of each shell evenly with salt; place upside down on paper towel to drain for 30 minutes.
4. In small nonstick skillet, heat 1 tablespoon of the oil over medium heat; add onion, garlic, fennel seeds, and red pepper flakes; cook about 5 minutes. Add sausage and cook until no longer pink, about 5 minutes; add reserved tomato pulp.
5. Stir in bran; fill each tomato with equal amounts of the sausage/bran mixture.
6. Place stuffed tomatoes in prepared pan; drizzle with remaining tablespoon oil.
7. Bake 20 to 30 minutes until top is lightly browned; remove with slotted spoon; place on bed of lettuce, if desired.

Basil-Oat "Fritters" with Tri-Color Peppers

Makes 4 servings.

A colorful presentation with glorious flavors—a vegetarian's dream! You can also serve the fritters alone for breakfast, topped with a poached egg.

Oat Bran (g): 25

Calories: 300   Total Fat (g): 21
Cholesterol (mg): 2   Sodium (mg): 322
Sat. Fat (g): 2   Fiber (g): 6

All counts are per serving

---

2 tablespoons olive oil
1 each red, yellow, and green bell pepper (about 1¼ pounds in all), seeded and sliced to ¼-inch-thick strips
1 medium onion, thinly sliced
¼ teaspoon salt

Fritters:
3 tablespoons oil
¾ cup oat bran
½ cup rolled oats
2 tablespoons grated Parmesan cheese
¼ teaspoon salt
¼ cup chopped fresh basil

1. In 12-inch nonstick skillet, heat oil over medium-high heat and sauté peppers and onion, with salt about 20 minutes, until tender and browned, stirring frequently. Place pepper mixture on plate, cover with foil to keep warm.
2. To prepare fritters, in same skillet, heat oil over high heat.
3. In medium saucepan, over high heat, combine oat bran, rolled oats, cheese, and salt with 1½ cups water; bring to a boil, stirring constantly until thickened, about 1 minute. Remove from heat; stir in basil.

4. Spoon oat mixture into skillet, making 4 fritters; cook 2 to 3 minutes on each side until well-browned.
5. With spatula, remove carefully from skillet; place each fritter on plate and top evenly with pepper mixture.

Sun-Dried Tomato and Mozzarella Tart
Makes 6 servings.

This rich, Mediterranean-style dish needs only Niçoise olives to make a satisfying cold-weather luncheon.

Oat Bran (g): 10

Calories: 278   Total Fat (g): 14
Cholesterol(mg): 50   Sodium (mg): 698
Sat. Fat (g): 3   Fiber (g): 3

All counts are per serving

Pastry:
½ cup all-purpose flour
½ cup oat bran
¼ cup oat flour
¼ teaspoon salt, optional

Pinch of granulated sugar
¼ cup chilled
    margarine, cut in
    pieces
3–4 tablespoons ice water

Filling:
One 16-ounce container
    lowfat (1%) cottage
    cheese
One 10-ounce package
    (thawed) frozen
    chopped spinach,
    drained and squeezed
1 cup shredded part-skim
    mozzarella

¼ cup chopped sun-dried
    tomatoes
2 tablespoons oat bran
2 tablespoons grated
    Parmesan cheese
1 large egg plus 1 egg
    white, lightly beaten
¼ teaspoon freshly
    ground pepper

1. To prepare pastry, in food processor fitted with steel blade, combine all dry ingredients; add margarine and pulse until mixture forms coarse crumbs.
2. Drizzle in water, 1 tablespoon at a time, pulsing until dough forms.
3. Shape dough into a ball and flatten; press dough into a 10-inch tart pan; refrigerate 30 minutes.
4. Preheat oven to 375° F.
5. Prick dough with a fork; bake 10 minutes; set aside.
6. To prepare filling, in large bowl, combine all ingredients; pour into prebaked crust.
7. Bake about 30 minutes, or until lightly browned. Let tart stand on rack 10 minutes before serving. Loosen edges with a knife.

Grilled Quail with
Brandied Sweet Potato Croquettes

Makes 4 servings.

Quail, each tiny bird weighing 3 to 4 ounces, is the perfect lunch portion. This dish is full of autumn flavor. Garnish with watercress and grapes for an elegant and stylish meal.

Oat Bran (g): 20

Calories: 512	Total Fat (g): 30
Cholesterol (mg): 68	Sodium (mg): 356
Sat. Fat (g): 6	Fiber (g): 5.5

All counts are per serving

Croquettes:

1 cup mashed cooked sweet potatoes	2 teaspoons brandy
¼ cup plus 3 tablespoons oat bran	¼ teaspoon salt
	⅛ teaspoon ground allspice
1 large egg, lightly beaten	3 tablespoons olive oil

Quail:

4 quail	¼ teaspoon salt
1 tablespoon olive oil	⅛ teaspoon freshly ground pepper
½ cup oat bran	
½ teaspoon crushed dried rosemary leaves	

1. To prepare croquettes, in medium bowl, combine sweet potatoes, ¼ cup of the oat bran, egg, brandy, salt and allspice; refrigerate, covered, 1½ hours.
2. On wax paper, divide mixture into 4 portions; gently form into 4-inch cylinders and roll in remaining oat bran, reserving any bran that is left over.

3. Place croquettes on rack for 10 minutes; carefully remove and roll in any remaining bran. Dry on rack 50 minutes.
4. In small nonstick skillet*, heat oil over high heat; brown croquettes, 2 at a time, on each side. Place on plate; cover with foil to keep warm.
5. Preheat broiler.
6. To prepare quail, with sharp scissors cut in half at breastbone; brush with oil.
7. In shallow dish, combine oat bran, rosemary, salt, and pepper; dredge each bird in mixture to coat.
8. Spray broiler rack with nonstick cooking spray; place quail skin side down on rack in pan 2 inches from heat. Broil 4 minutes; turn and broil 1 minute longer, until browned.

*Use a *small* skillet so that less oil is needed and croquettes will brown more quickly and evenly.

Garden Vegetable Muffins

Makes 12 muffins.

This garden medley muffin adds a colorful touch when served with cottage cheese or soup.

Oat Bran (g): 9

Calories: 173   Total Fat (g): 6
Cholesterol (mg): 23   Sodium (mg): 223
Sat. Fat (g): < 1   Fiber (g): 29

All counts are per serving

---

1 1/2 cups all-purpose flour
1/2 cup oat flour
1/2 cup oat bran
1/2 cup rolled oats
3 tablespoons granulated sugar
2 teaspoons baking powder
1/2 teaspoon baking soda

1/2 teaspoon salt
1 1/4 cups skim milk
1/4 cup vegetable oil
1 large egg at room temperature
3/4 cup frozen peas and carrots (thawed)
1 black radish or 2 large red radishes, grated

1. Preheat oven to 325° F.; line 12 muffin cups with paper liners or spray cups with nonstick cooking spray.
2. In large bowl, combine all dry ingredients.
3. In small bowl, combine milk, oil, and egg; add to dry ingredients, mixing with fork until just combined. Stir in vegetables.
4. Divide batter evenly among prepared cups.
5. Bake about 35 minutes, or until toothpick inserted in center comes out clean.
6. Turn muffins onto rack to cool.

Smoked Chicken Salad on Wild Greens with Balsamic Vinaigrette

Makes 4 servings.

Jicama adds a delightful crunch to this salad, bathed in naturally sweet balsamic vinegar. If jicama is not available, use water chestnuts as substitute.

Oat Bran (g): 21

Calories: 492   Total Fat (g): 35
Cholesterol (mg): 25   Sodium (mg): 595
Sat. Fat (g): 5   Fiber (g): 6

All counts are per serving

Vinaigrette:
1/2 cup extra virgin olive oil
1/4 cup balsamic vinegar
1 teaspoon grated orange peel
1/4 teaspoon freshly ground pepper
salt to taste, optional

Salad:
1 1/4 cups rolled oats
8 ounces smoked chicken (or turkey) cut in julienne strips
1/2 cup each small red and green seedless grapes
1/2 cup chopped pared jicama
1/4 cup sliced almonds
4 cups wild greens (arugula, mâche, frisée, dandelion)

1. To prepare vinaigrette, in small bowl whisk all ingredients; set aside.
2. In large skillet, over medium heat, toast oats 5 to 7 minutes until lightly browned, stirring frequently.
3. To prepare salad, combine chicken, oats, grapes, *jicama*, and almonds in large bowl; whisk vinaigrette and stir into salad.
4. Garnish 4 plates with wild greens; spoon equal amounts of salad onto each plate.

Warm Lentils with Lemon Vinaigrette
Makes 4 servings.

When these lentils are served with thin slices of leftover lamb, can Spring be far behind!

Oat Bran (g): 21

Calories: 515	Total Fat (g): 29
Cholesterol (mg): 0	Sodium (mg): 389
Sat. Fat (g): 3	Fiber (g): 9

All counts are per serving

1¼ cups rolled oats
1 cup dried lentils
1 packet onion bouillon
½ cup cherry tomatoes, quartered
3 scallions, sliced
1 rib celery, diced
¼ cup chopped fresh parsley
Radicchio leaves to garnish, optional

Vinaigrette:
¼ cup each hazelnut oil and olive oil
¼ cup fresh lemon juice
¼ teaspoon salt

1. In large skillet, over medium heat, toast oats 5 to 7 minutes until lightly browned, stirring frequently.
2. To prepare lentils, rinse and discard any pebbles you may find.
3. In medium saucepan, over medium heat, combine lentils, bouillon, and 2 cups of water; bring to a boil. Reduce heat; cover and simmer 25 to 35 minutes until tender; adding more water if necessary.
4. To prepare vinaigrette, in small saucepan, over low heat, whisk together all ingredients until warm.
5. Place lentils in large bowl. Add oats, tomatoes, scallions, celery, and parsley. Pour warm dressing over mixture; stir to combine.
6. Serve immediately.

Soups

Dilled Cream of Carrot Soup (Microwave)
Makes 4 servings.

Rich and delicious. Buttermilk enriches and thickens this soup without adding fat.

Oat Bran (g): 16

Calories: 244   Total Fat (g): 11
Cholesterol (mg): 4   Sodium (mg): 713
Sat. Fat (g): 1   Fiber (g): 7

All counts are per serving

---

1 medium onion, chopped	¾ cup oat bran
2 tablespoons olive oil	1 teaspoon granulated sugar
5 cups sliced carrots	1 tablespoon chopped fresh dill, or 1 teaspoon dried
1 13¾-ounce can chicken broth	
1½ cups buttermilk	

1. In 3-quart microwave-safe casserole, combine onion and oil. Microwave on High 2 minutes.
2. Add carrots and ½ cup of the chicken broth; cover and vent. Microwave on High 12 to 14 minutes, until carrots are tender, stirring once. Purée in food processor.
3. Return mixture to casserole; stir in remaining broth, buttermilk, oat bran, and sugar. Cover, microwave on High 4 to 6 minutes, until boiling. (For a thinner consistency, add more chicken broth.)
4. Stir in dill; serve immediately.*

Mom's Barley Soup

Makes 4 servings.

Served with a salad and a crusty loaf of bread, this hearty soup makes a satisfying country supper. An added bonus: the barley provides an extra dose of heart-healthy soluble fiber.

Oat Bran (g): 17

Calories: 327   Total Fat (g): 11
Cholesterol (mg): 26   Sodium (mg): 603
Sat. Fat (g): 3   Fiber (g): 7

All counts are per serving

---

*Do not reheat; the texture becomes gelatinous.

1   cup rolled oats
1/2 cup medium barley
2   tablespoons vegetable
     oil
1   pound lamb necks*,
     trimmed of fat
1   medium onion, chopped
2   carrots, chopped
1   rib celery, chopped

1   leek, white part only,
     washed and sliced
2   cups sliced
     mushrooms (about 4
     ounces)
1   13³/₄-ounce can beef
     broth
1/4 teaspoon dried thyme
1   bay leaf
     salt to taste, optional

1. In Dutch oven, over medium heat, toast oats and barley about 5 minutes, stirring frequently; remove and set aside.
2. In Dutch oven, heat oil over medium-high heat; sauté lamb necks, browning on all sides; remove with a slotted spoon; set aside.
3. Add onion, carrots, celery, leek; cook 5 minutes, stirring frequently; add mushrooms, cook 5 minutes longer.
4. Pour in broth and 3 cups water; add thyme, bay leaf, and browned lamb; bring to a boil; reduce heat and simmer 10 minutes.
5. Remove lamb necks with slotted spoon; cool and remove meat from bone.
6. Add boned lamb, rolled oats and barley to Dutch oven; simmer 30 minutes, adding more liquid if necessary.

*Lamb neck is very tasty; 1/3 pound boneless lamb stew meat may be used instead.

Spinach Soup with Herb Dumplings
Makes 6 servings of 2 dumplings per serving.

A super start for the evening meal. This is a quick soup for cold days. The dumplings are made in the time it takes for the soup to come to a boil.

Oat Bran (g): 14	
Calories: 201	Total Fat: (g): 9
Cholesterol (mg): < 1	Sodium (mg): 491
Sat. Fat (g): < 1	Fiber (g): 3
All counts are per serving	

1 tablespoon vegetable oil
1 medium onion, chopped
6 cups unsalted chicken broth
1/2 teaspoon salt
Freshly ground pepper to taste
1 cup fresh spinach, shredded
1 cup Bisquick
1 cup oat bran
2/3 cup skim milk
1/2 teaspoon dried marjoram

1. In Dutch oven, heat oil over medium heat; sauté onion 3 minutes until tender.
2. Add chicken broth, spinach, salt and pepper; bring to a boil over medium heat.
3. In medium bowl, combine Bisquick, oat bran, milk, and marjoram; mix with a fork until soft dough forms.
4. Drop by rounded tablespoons into boiling soup; reduce heat; cook, uncovered, 10 minutes; cover and cook 10 minutes longer.

Main Dishes

South of the Border Pizza

Makes 4 servings.

Very spicy and delicious.

Oat Bran (g): 15

Calories: 344   Total Fat (g): 18
Cholesterol (mg): 19   Sodium (mg): 522
Sat. Fat (g): 1   Fiber (g): 4.5

All counts are per serving

Dough:
3/4 cup all-purpose flour
1/4 cup oat flour
1/2 cup oat bran
1 package active dry yeast
1/2 teaspoon granulated sugar

1/2 teaspoon salt
2 tablespoons vegetable oil
1/2 cup warm water (120°–130° F.)

Topping:

1 1/2 cups mild salsa (no salt added)*

1/2 cup sliced pitted black olives

1 small jalapeño pepper, finely chopped**

3/4 cup shredded Monterey Jack cheese

1. To prepare dough, in food processor fitted with steel blade, combine flours, oat bran, yeast, sugar, and salt.
2. With machine running, add oil and water; when dough gathers into a ball, pulse 20 times to knead.
3. Spray medium bowl with nonstick cooking spray. Place dough in prepared bowl; turn to coat top surface. Cover with plastic wrap and let rise in a warm, draft-free place until doubled in size, about 30 minutes.
4. Preheat oven to 425° F. Spray 12-inch pizza pan with nonstick cooking spray.
5. Punch down dough and place in center of prepared pan. With fingers, press dough into a 12-inch circle.
6. Spread salsa over dough to within 1/2 inch of edge. Sprinkle olives, pepper, and cheese evenly on top.
7. Bake 25 to 30 minutes, until crust is browned and crisp.

*Available in health food stores.
**For a less spicy pizza, eliminate jalapeño pepper.

Shrimp Ragout (Microwave)
Makes 4 servings.

Serve over Garlicky Hot Groats (p. 72).

Oat Bran (g): 10

Calories: 318   Total Fat (g): 10
Cholesterol (mg): 174 Sodium (mg): 646
Sat. Fat (g): 1   Fiber (g): 3.5

All counts are per serving

1¼ pounds small shrimp (about 40)
Juice of half a lemon
2 tablespoons olive oil
2 garlic cloves, crushed
One 28-ounce can crushed tomatoes with added purée
One 15-ounce can tomato sauce (no salt added)
½ cup dry red wine
½ teaspoon salt
½ teaspoon dried oregano
⅛ teaspoon cayenne pepper
½ cup oat bran

1. Peel and devein shrimp; place in water with lemon juice. Drain and dry shrimp with paper towels; set aside.
2. In a 3-quart microwave-safe casserole, combine oil and garlic; microwave on High 2 minutes.
3. Add remaining ingredients except shrimp and oat bran; microwave on High 10 minutes, stirring once. Add oat bran gradually, stirring constantly to avoid lumping. Microwave on High 2 minutes longer.
4. Add shrimp; microwave on High 3 to 5 minutes, stirring once, until shrimp are firm and opaque.

Sweet and Sour Turkey Meatballs
Makes 4 servings.

Serve with brown rice or cellophane noodles and a green vegetable.

Oat Bran (g): 16

Calories: 470   Total Fat (g): 17
Cholesterol (mg): 164   Sodium (mg): 677
Sat. Fat (g): 6   Fiber (g): 4

All counts are per serving

---

1 1/4 pounds ground turkey
3/4 cup oat bran
1 large egg, lightly beaten with 1/4 cup water
1 tablespoon chopped fresh cilantro
1/4 teaspoon each salt and ground cloves
3 tablespoons Brownulated light brown sugar
2 teaspoons cornstarch
One 20-ounce can crushed pineapple in juice, drained, reserving 3/4 cup of the juice
1/4 cup cider vinegar
1/3 cup ketchup
1 tablespoon reduced-sodium soy sauce
1 garlic clove, minced
1/4 pound snow peas

1. In large bowl, combine turkey, oat bran, egg mixture, cilantro, salt, and cloves. Shape mixture into 20 meatballs.
2. In 12-inch nonstick skillet sprayed with nonstick cooking spray, cook meatballs over medium heat for 5 minutes, or until browned; remove; add sugar and cornstarch to skillet; whisk in reserved pineapple juice, vinegar, ketchup, soy sauce, and garlic, stirring constantly, until cornstarch is dissolved.
3. Bring to a boil; cook, stirring, until thickened, about 1 minute.
4. Add meatballs, pineapple, and snow peas, stirring to coat with sauce; reduce heat. Cover and simmer 12 to 15 minutes, or until turkey is cooked, turning meatballs once.

Pasta with Chick Peas and Spinach Pesto
Makes 4 servings.

A meatless dish fit for Popeye! The chick peas are a nutritional plus, providing extra soluble fiber. Try serving this with a tomato and red onion salad.

Oat Bran (g): 16

Calories: 587   Total Fat (g): 30
Cholesterol (mg): 0   Sodium (mg): 388
Sat. Fat (g): 4   Fiber (g): 5.5

All counts are per serving

---

2 cups packed spinach leaves, washed and drained
1 small shallot
1/2 teaspoon salt
1/4 teaspoon freshly ground pepper
3/4 cup oat bran
1/2 cup extra virgin olive oil
8 ounces fusilli macaroni
One 8-ounce can chick peas, drained

1. To prepare spinach pesto: in food processor fitted with steel blade, process first 4 ingredients until spinach is finely chopped; add oat bran and pulse until combined.
2. With machine running, add oil, scraping mixture down sides of bowl; set aside.
3. In large pot of rapidly boiling water, cook fusilli 10 to 12 minutes, until tender; drain, reserving 3/4 cup water.
4. In large bowl, combine pasta, chick peas, spinach pesto, and reserved water. Serve immediately.

Crunchy Baked Chicken

Makes 4 servings.

To make this dinner complete, serve with baked potatoes and baby carrots.

Oat Bran (g): 10

Calories: 250   Total Fat (g): 10
Cholesterol (mg): 67   Sodium (mg): 415
Sat. Fat (g): 2   Fiber (g): 2

All counts are per serving

---

2   tablespoons unsalted margarine
One 2½ to 3-pound broiler or fryer chicken, cut in parts, skin removed and trimmed of excess fat
1½ cups Kellogg's Common Sense Oat Bran

3   tablespoons oat bran
1   tablespoon finely chopped fresh sage, or 1 teaspoon dried
¼ teaspoon salt
¼ teaspoon freshly ground pepper
½ cup lowfat yogurt
1   tablespoon spicy brown mustard

1. Preheat oven to 350° F. Melt margarine in 9- x 13-inch baking dish in oven; remove dish. Rinse and dry chicken.
2. In sealable plastic bag, combine Kellogg's Oat Bran, oat bran, sage, salt, and pepper; crush with a rolling pin; place on wax paper.
3. In cup, combine yogurt and mustard; brush each piece of chicken with mixture; *sprinkle* with oat bran mixture to coat.
4. Place chicken, meaty side up, in prepared dish; bake 1 hour, until juices run clear when meat is pricked with a fork.

Three-Cheese Lasagna
Makes 8 servings.

This hearty meal may be prepared ahead of time and frozen. To reheat, place in 350° F. oven for 1½ hours.

Oat Bran (g): 13

Calories: 526   Total Fat (g): 20
Cholesterol (mg): 57   Sodium (mg): 678
Sat. Fat (g): 9   Fiber (g): 5

All counts are per serving

---

2   tablespoons olive oil
1   carrot, finely diced
1   rib celery, finely diced
1   small onion, chopped
2   garlic cloves, minced
Two 28-ounce cans Italian-style tomatoes (no salt added)
One 8-ounce can tomato sauce
½   teaspoon salt
½   teaspoon crushed red pepper flakes
12   sheets curly lasagna noodles
One 2-pound container part-skim ricotta cheese
One 8-ounce package part-skim mozzarella cheese, shredded, reserving ¼ cup
½   cup grated Romano cheese
¼   cup chopped fresh basil
1¼   cups oat bran

1. To prepare sauce, in Dutch oven, heat 1 tablespoon of the oil over medium-high heat; sauté carrot, celery, onion, and garlic 3 to 5 minutes, until tender, stirring frequently.
2. Add tomatoes and tomato sauce, salt and pepper flakes, crush tomatoes with a potato masher; reduce heat to medium and cook 45 minutes, stirring occasionally.

3. Preheat oven to 350° F.
4. Add remaining tablespoon oil to large pot of boiling water; cook noodles 8 to 10 minutes, until almost tender; drain.
5. In large bowl, combine ricotta, mozzarella, grated Romano, and basil.
6. In 9- x 13-inch baking dish, alternately layer noodles, cheese, oat bran, and sauce, ending top layer with sauce and remaining mozzarella.
7. Bake 1 hour; remove from oven and let stand 10 minutes before serving.

Baked Snapper with
Julienne of Vegetables

Makes 4 servings.

Easy and elegant—serve vegetables and sauce over groats
for extra fiber.

Oat Bran (g): 10

Calories: 219   Total Fat (g): 6
Cholesterol (mg): 45   Sodium (mg): 257
Sat. Fat (g): 1   Fiber (g): 3

All counts are per serving

---

1   cup julienne strips of
    carrot
1   cup julienne strips of
    leek, washed, white
    part only
1/2 cup chicken broth
1/4 cup dry white wine
2   tablespoons half-and-
    half
1/4 teaspoon crushed dried
    tarragon
Salt and pepper to taste
1/2 cup oat bran
3/4 teaspoon salt-free
    lemon and herb
    seasoning blend
1   pound snapper fillets
2   teaspoons vegetable oil

1. Preheat oven to 400° F.
2. Place carrot, leek, broth, wine, half-and-half, tarra-
   gon, and salt and pepper in 7½- x 11¾-inch baking
   dish; cover with foil and bake 10 minutes.
3. In a bowl, combine oat bran and no-salt seasoning
   blend; dredge each fillet in oat bran mixture.
4. Sprinkle remaining oat bran mixture evenly over vegetables; place fillets on top, overlapping if necessary;
   drizzle with oil.
5. Bake, uncovered, 20 to 25 minutes, or until fish flakes
   easily with a fork.

Chili Pot Pie with Pepper Crust
Makes 4 servings.

A Tex-Mex taste treat in one dish.

Oat Bran (g): 16

Calories: 620   Total Fat (g): 29
Cholesterol (mg): 66   Sodium (mg): 370
Sat. Fat (g): 5   Fiber (g): 12

All counts are per serving

Filling:
2 tablespoons vegetable oil

2 medium onions, chopped

1 garlic clove, crushed

1 pound trimmed boneless beef round, cut into 1-inch cubes

1/4 cup oat bran

1/2 teaspoon salt

1/2 teaspoon chili powder

3 medium carrots, thinly sliced

1 medium green bell pepper, seeded and chopped

12 ounces beer

1 teaspoon ground cumin

One 15 1/2-ounce can kidney beans, drained

Crust:
1/2 cup all-purpose flour

1/2 cup oat bran

1/2 teaspoon black peppercorns, crushed

1/4 teaspoon salt

1/3 cup chilled margarine, cut in pieces

1-2 tablespoons ice water

1. To prepare filling, in Dutch oven, heat oil over medium-high heat; sauté onions and garlic 3 to 5 minutes until tender, stirring occasionally.
2. Add beef; brown on all sides.

3. In small bowl, combine oat bran, salt, and chili powder; sprinkle over beef mixture; toss to combine.
4. Add remaining filling ingredients, except beans; stir to combine.
5. Bring to a boil; reduce heat, cover, and simmer about 1 hour, until beef is tender.
6. Stir in beans; turn heat to high and cook, uncovered, 10 minutes, stirring frequently.
7. Remove from heat; spoon chili mixture into 1½-quart casserole, 8 inches in diameter.
8. To prepare crust, in food processor fitted with steel blade, combine all dry ingredients; add margarine and process until mixture forms coarse crumbs. Add water, 1 tablespoon at a time; process until dough forms.
9. Shape dough into a ball; flatten and wrap in plastic wrap; refrigerate 30 minutes.
10. Preheat oven to 425° F.
11. On lightly floured surface, roll dough into 9-inch circle*; fold in half and lift with spatula onto mixture, unfold.
12. Crimp edges to seal around rim of dish; cut four 1-inch slits with a knife.
13. Bake 30 minutes, or until golden.

*Roll dough 1 inch larger than diameter of casserole. This dough is crumbly, but because of fat content can be pinched together carefully if it breaks.

Turkey Meatloaf

Makes 6 servings.

"Diner Food" update! Serve with lumpy mashed potatoes and peas for a heart-warming, home-style meal.

Oat Bran (g): 11

Calories: 316	Total Fat (g): 14
Cholesterol (mg): 168	Sodium (mg): 585
Sat. Fat (g): 5	Fiber (g): 2

All counts are per serving

---

1 cup rolled oats
1 cup ketchup with onions
2 large eggs
1 tablespoon chopped
  fresh parsley

1   garlic clove, minced
1/8 teaspoon freshly
  ground pepper
1/2 cup skim milk
1 1/2 pounds ground turkey

1. Preheat oven to 350° F.; spray 8 1/2- x 4 1/2- x 2 1/2-inch loaf pan with nonstick cooking spray; set aside.
2. In large bowl, combine all ingredients except turkey. Add turkey; work lightly with fingers to combine.
3. Place in pan; bake 1 hour.

Roast Chicken with Sherry Stuffing
Makes 6 servings.

This is a simple dish, rich in flavor and oat bran, that uses a no-cook stuffing.

Oat Bran (g): 14

Calories: 504
Cholesterol (mg): 133
Sat. Fat (g): 7

Total Fat (g): 25
Sodium (mg): 472
Fiber (g): 3

All counts are per serving

1/4 cup dried currants	1 cup oat bran
1/4 cup dry sherry	1/2 cup finely chopped mushrooms
One 4–5-pound roasting chicken	1 medium onion, finely chopped
Salt and pepper to taste	1/2 cup egg substitute
2 slices day-old or slightly toasted bread, cut into 1/4-inch cubes	1 teaspoon dried savory
	3/4 teaspoon salt

1. In large bowl, combine currants and sherry, set aside.
2. Preheat oven to 350° F.
3. Remove giblets from chicken; reserve for other use. Wash and pat chicken dry with paper towels. Season cavities with salt and pepper; set aside.
4. To prepare stuffing, combine remaining ingredients in same bowl with currant mixture.
5. Fill cavities of chicken with stuffing; truss or skewer closed.
6. Place chicken on rack, breast side up, in roasting pan; roast about 2 hours, or until juices run clear when inner thigh is pricked with fork.
7. Let stand 15 minutes before carving.

Wontons in Soy-Ginger Sauce

Makes 4 servings of 5 each.

These wontons will be the envy of your local Chinese restaurant. Serve with a colorful dish of stir-fried vegetables.

Oat Bran (g): 19

Calories: 518   Total Fat (g): 18
Cholesterol (mg): 0   Sodium (mg): 882
Sat. Fat (g): 2   Fiber (g): 4.5

All counts are per serving

Filling:

One 15-ounce can straw mushrooms*, drained (¼ cup chopped and reserved)

¾ cup mashed drained tofu

½ cup each oat bran and rolled oats

3 tablespoons sesame oil

1 teaspoon chili paste with garlic*

40 wonton skins* (thawed if frozen)

Sauce:

¼ cup reduced-sodium soy sauce

2 tablespoons dark brown sugar

1 tablespoon toasted sesame seeds

2 teaspoons minced fresh ginger root

2 scallions, thinly sliced

1 tablespoon vegetable oil

1. To prepare filling, in medium bowl combine the ¼ cup reserved chopped mushrooms, tofu, oat bran and rolled oats, sesame oil, and chili paste.
2. Place 1 rounded tablespoon of tofu mixture in the

*Available at Oriental markets.

center of each of 20 wontons; with a pastry brush dipped in water, moisten edges of wontons.

3. Place 1 of the remaining wontons over each; press edges together with a fork.

4. Cover stuffed wontons with damp paper towels.

5. To prepare sauce, in small sauce pan, over medium heat, combine all ingredients with $1/2$ cup water; bring to a boil. Remove from heat, add remaining mushrooms; keep warm.

6. Add oil to a large pot of rapidly boiling water; add wontons and cook 4 minutes. Remove with a slotted spoon to serving platter; spoon sauce over wontons.

Two-Grain Trout

Makes 4 servings.

Ginger adds a taste of the tropics to this Idaho favorite.

Oat Bran (g): 15

Calories: 372   Total Fat (g): 17
Cholesterol (mg): 79   Sodium (mg): 346
Sat. Fat (g): 3   Fiber (g): 4

All counts are per serving

---

³/₄   cup steel-cut oats
¹/₄   cup bulgur wheat
Two 12-ounce whole
      dressed trout (boned,
      head removed)
2   tablespoons oat flour

¹/₂ teaspoon each cayenne
    pepper, ground cumin,
    nutmeg, and ginger
¹/₂ cup sliced scallions
1   teaspoon grated fresh
    ginger root
¹/₂ teaspoon salt
2   tablespoons olive oil

1. In medium saucepan, combine oats and bulgur wheat with just enough water to cover; bring to a boil over high heat; remove from heat. Let stand, covered, 10 minutes, until water is absorbed.
2. Preheat oven to 350° F.; spray 7¹/₂- x 11³/₄-inch baking dish with nonstick cooking spray.
3. Rinse fish and pat dry with paper towels, place in prepared pan.
4. In small bowl, combine oat flour and spices; rub fish inside and out with oat mixture.
5. In medium bowl, combine oat/bulgur mixture, scallions, ginger root, and salt; spoon equal amounts into cavities of fish. Close with twine, drizzle with the oil.
6. Bake, uncovered about 25 minutes, until fish flakes easily.

Rum-Raisin-Stuffed Pork Chops

Makes 4 servings.

Elegant enough for a New Year's Eve dinner.

Oat Bran (g): 13

Calories: 512   Total Fat: (g): 22
Cholesterol (mg): 76   Sodium (mg): 170
Sat. Fat (g): 5   Fiber (g): 5

All counts are per serving

---

3 tablespoons vegetable oil
1 rib celery, finely chopped
1 small onion, finely chopped
1/4 cup dark rum
1 slice day-old or slightly toasted bread, cut into 1/4-inch cubes
1/2 cup Kellogg's Common Sense Oat Bran
2 tablespoons chopped fresh parsley
1/2 teaspoon salt
4 rib pork chops, 1 1/2 inches thick (2–2 1/4 pounds) trimmed of fat, each slit horizontally to rib
1/2 cup oat bran
One 20-ounce can crushed pineapple in juice, drained, reserve juice
1/4 cup dark raisins

1. Preheat oven to 350° F.; spray 7 1/2- x 11 3/4-inch baking dish with nonstick cooking spray; set aside.
2. To prepare stuffing, in 12-inch nonstick skillet, over medium heat, heat 2 tablespoons of the oil; sauté celery and onion 3 to 5 minutes, until tender, stirring occasionally; add rum and cook 2 minutes.
3. Add bread cubes; stir to combine. Stir in Kellogg's Oat Bran, parsley, and salt; cook 2 minutes.
4. Fill pockets of each chop with 1/4 cup of the stuffing; fasten each chop together with 2 wooden toothpicks.

5. On wax paper, dredge each chop in oat bran, reserving any bran not used.
6. In same skillet, heat remaining oil over medium heat; brown pork chops 5 minutes on each side; remove and place in prepared dish.
7. Add 2 tablespoons reserved pineapple juice to skillet, scraping sides and bottom with wooden spoon; pour over chops in dish.
8. In small bowl, combine pineapple, remaining juice, remaining oat bran, and raisins, spoon over chops.
9. Cover dish tightly with foil; bake 1 hour, or until chops are tender and thoroughly cooked. Remove toothpicks before serving.

Vegetables, Grains, and Side Dishes

"Oven Fried" Onion Rings

Makes 4 servings.

Low in fat, high in flavor!

Oat Bran (g): 26

Calories: 241	Total Fat (g): 14
Cholesterol (mg): 68	Sodium (mg): 179
Sat. Fat (g): 1	Fiber (g): 5

All counts are per serving

---

1 large Bermuda onion, cut into 1/4-inch-thick slices, separated into rings
1 large egg
2 large egg whites

1 1/4 cups oat bran
1/4 teaspoon each paprika and cayenne pepper
1/4 teaspoon salt
3 tablespoons vegetable oil

1. Preheat oven to 450° F. Spray cookie sheet with non-stick cooking spray; set aside.
2. In a shallow dish, beat egg and egg whites with a fork.

3. In a small bowl, combine oat bran, spices, and salt; place half of mixture in sealable plastic bag.
4. Dip onion rings into egg, adding a few at a time to bag; shake to coat; repeat with remaining oat bran mixture.
5. Place rings on prepared sheet; drizzle evenly with the oil.
6. Bake 15 to 20 minutes, turning once, or until golden brown.

Garlicky Oat Groats

Makes 8 ¹/₂ cup servings.

For a milder flavor substitute shallots for the garlic.

Oat Bran (g): 17

Calories: 104   Total Fat (g): 5
Cholesterol (mg): 0   Sodium (mg): 10
Sat. Fat (g): <1   Fiber (g): 2

All counts are per serving

---

2 tablespoons olive oil   2 cups oat groats, rinsed
2 ribs celery, finely   and drained
   chopped   ¹/₂ teaspoon salt, optional
3 large garlic cloves,
   minced

1. In Dutch oven, heat oil over medium-high heat; sauté celery and garlic 3 to 5 minutes, stirring frequently.
2. Add groats; sauté 5 minutes, stirring frequently until lightly browned.
3. Add 4 cups water, bring to a boil. Cover, reduce heat, and simmer about 45 minutes, until water is absorbed. Season with salt, if desired.

Metro Macaroni and Cheese
Makes 4 servings.

A comforting dish for "kids" of all ages.

Oat Bran (g): 9

Calories: 514   Total Fat (g): 16
Cholesterol (mg): 38   Sodium (mg): 730
Sat. Fat (g): 7   Fiber (g): 4

All counts are per serving

1⅓ cups Kellogg's
    Common Sense Oat
    Bran
8   ounces elbow
    macaroni
3   tablespoons reduced-
    calorie tub
    margarine, melted
1¼ cups skim milk
1½ teaspoons
    Worcestershire sauce

1   teaspoon dry mustard
½   teaspoon salt
⅛   teaspoon cayenne
    pepper
One 8-ounce package
    reduced-fat shredded
    sharp Cheddar
    cheese (2 cups)
2   tablespoons oat bran

1. Preheat oven to 350° F. Spray a 2-quart casserole with nonstick cooking spray; set aside.
2. In sealable plastic bag, crush Kellogg's Oat Bran with rolling pin.
3. In medium pot of rapidly boiling water, cook macaroni 9 to 12 minutes, until tender; drain. Add to casserole with 1 tablespoon of the margarine.
4. In small saucepan, over medium heat, combine milk, Worcestershire sauce, mustard, salt, and pepper; simmer 5 minutes; stir into macaroni with 1½ cups of the Cheddar cheese and oat bran.
5. In medium bowl, combine remaining ½ cup cheese, margarine, and crushed oat bran; sprinkle over casserole.
6. Bake 20 to 25 minutes, until crispy.

Cauliflower Bombay (Microwave)

Makes 4 servings.

A flavorful and colorful dish to accompany meat, fish, or poultry.

Oat Bran (g): 5

Calories: 149	Total Fat (g): 8
Cholesterol (mg): 0	Sodium (mg): 438
Sat. Fat (g): < 1	Fiber (g): 4.5

All counts are per serving

---

4 small onions, thinly sliced
2 tablespoons vegetable oil
2 teaspoons peeled fresh ginger root, minced
2 tablespoons oat bran
2 teaspoons mustard seeds
1 teaspoon cumin seeds, crushed
1 teaspoon turmeric
1/2 teaspoon salt
1/4 teaspoon freshly ground pepper
4 cups fresh cauliflowerets (about a 1 3/4-pound head)
1/4 cup chicken broth or water
1/2 cup Kellogg's Common Sense Oat Bran

1. In 7 1/2- x 11 3/4-inch microwave safe baking dish, combine onions, 1 tablespoon of the oil, and ginger; microwave on High 5 minutes, stirring once.
2. In cup, combine oat bran, mustard seeds, cumin seeds, turmeric, salt, and pepper.
3. Add cauliflower to baking dish; combine with spice mixture; pour broth over casserole.
4. Cover with vented plastic wrap; microwave on High 8 to 11 minutes, or until tender, stirring twice.
5. Preheat broiler.
6. In sealable plastic bag, with rolling pin, crush Kellogg's Common Sense Oat Bran.

7. Sprinkle crushed bran on top of cauliflower mixture; drizzle with remaining tablespoon oil.
8. Broil 4 inches from heat, 1 to 2 minutes, until browned.

Corn Creole

Makes 4 servings.

A New Orleans-inspired dish that adds color to any meal.

Oat Bran (g): 5

Calories: 136   Total Fat (g): 5
Cholesterol (mg): 0   Sodium (mg): 384
Sat. Fat (g): < 1   Fiber (g): 3.5

All counts are per serving

---

2 *medium tomatoes or 2 cups chopped, drained canned tomatoes*	*¹/₈ teaspoon cayenne pepper*
1 *tablespoon olive oil*	*One 10-ounce package frozen corn kernels, thawed*
¹/₂ medium green bell pepper, seeded and chopped	*¹/₂ cup spicy vegetable juice*
1 *small onion, chopped*	*¹/₄ cup oat bran*
¹/₂ teaspoon salt	

1. Place whole tomatoes in small saucepan of boiling water 30 seconds; cool slightly, peel and chop, set aside.
2. In 12-inch nonstick skillet, heat oil over medium heat; sauté pepper and onion 3 minutes; add tomatoes and pepper and cook 3 minutes longer.
3. Stir in corn, vegetable juice, and oat bran; cook 3 minutes, stirring occasionally.

Broccoli Oat Torta

Makes 4 servings.

Oats turned elegant with a middle layer of broccoli and cheese. Perfect with fall game dishes.

Oat Bran (g): 21

Calories: 206
Cholesterol (mg): 27
Sat. Fat (g): 5

Total Fat (g): 11
Sodium (mg): 469
Fiber (g): 4.5

All counts are per serving

---

1 cup oat bran
1/2 teaspoon salt
1/8 teaspoon ground
   nutmeg
One 10-ounce package
   frozen chopped
   broccoli, thawed,
   reserve 1/4 cup

4 ounces Muenster
   cheese, shredded,
   reserving 1/4 cup
1/2 teaspoon grated lemon
   peel
1/4 teaspoon freshly
   ground pepper

1. Preheat oven to 325° F.; spray a 6-cup soufflé dish with nonstick cooking spray; set aside.
2. In medium saucepan, over high heat, combine oat bran, salt, and nutmeg with 3 1/2 cups water; bring to a boil, cook 1 minute, stirring occasionally.
3. Remove from heat; cook about 5 minutes, until thickened.
4. In paper towels, squeeze broccoli of excess water. Pour half the oats into prepared dish; spoon broccoli over layer and sprinkle with cheese, lemon peel, and pepper.
5. Pour remaining oats over broccoli and cheese to cover; garnish with reserved broccoli and cheese.
6. Bake 30 minutes; let stand 5 minutes before serving.

Wild Rice and Oat Pilaf

Makes 4 servings.

A hint of orange flavor makes this a perfect pilaf to serve with duck.

Oat Bran (g): 13

Calories: 265   Total Fat (g): 13
Cholesterol (mg): 0   Sodium (mg): 565
Sat. Fat (g): 1   Fiber (g): 4.5

All counts are per serving

---

³/₄ cup rolled oats   *¹/₂ cup wild rice*
2 tablespoons olive oil   *One 13³/₄-ounce can beef*
2 medium carrots, diced   *   broth*
1 medium onion, finely   *¹/₄ cup chopped pecans*
*   chopped*   *2   teaspoons grated*
                               *   orange peel*

1. In Dutch oven, over medium heat, toast oats 5 to 7 minutes, stirring frequently until lightly browned. Remove oats and set aside.
2. In same pan, heat oil over high heat; sauté carrots and onion 5 minutes, stirring constantly.
3. Add wild rice to pan; cook 1 minute; stirring constantly.
4. Add broth with 1 cup water; bring to a boil. Cover; reduce heat and simmer 45 to 55 minutes, until rice is done but chewy.
5. Remove from heat; stir in oats, pecans, and orange peel; let stand, covered, 10 minutes.

Double Oat, Potato, and Turnip Gratin
Makes 4 servings.

If you're not a turnip lover, skip them and double up on the potatoes instead.

Oat Bran (g): 7

Calories: 215   Total Fat (g): 1
Cholesterol (mg): 4   Sodium (mg): 551
Sat. Fat (g): < 1   Fiber (g): 5

All counts are per serving

---

3   medium baking
    potatoes (about 1
    pound) pared and
    thinly sliced
3   medium turnips (about
    1 pound) pared and
    thinly sliced
3/4 cup Kellogg's Common
    Sense Oat Bran

3   tablespoons oat bran
1/2 teaspoon salt
One 12-ounce can
    evaporated skim milk
2   teaspoons grated
    Parmesan cheese
1/2 teaspoon paprika

1. Preheat oven to 375° F.; spray 7- x 11-inch baking dish with nonstick cooking spray.
2. In prepared dish, layer 1/3 of the potatoes and turnips; sprinkle with 1/3 of the Kellogg's Oat Bran, oat bran, and salt.
3. Repeat with 2 more layers; pour milk over all and sprinkle cheese and paprika over the top.
4. Cover with foil; bake 30 minutes. Remove foil; bake 30 minutes longer, or until lightly browned and tender. Let stand 5 minutes before serving.

Potato Pancakes

Makes 6 servings.

For an occasional treat, serve with crème fraîche instead of applesauce. Can be made ahead and reheated.

Oat Bran (g): 9

Calories: 205   Total Fat (g): 11
Cholesterol (mg): 46   Sodium (mg): 208
Sat. Fat (g): 1   Fiber (g): 3

All counts are per serving

---

3 large baking potatoes,   *²/₃ cup oat bran*
pared, grated, and   *¹/₂ teaspoon salt*
drained   *¹/₄ teaspoon pepper*
1 medium onion, grated   *¹/₄ cup vegetable oil*
1 large egg plus 1 large
egg white, lightly beaten

1. In large bowl, combine potatoes, onion, egg and egg white combination, oat bran, salt, and pepper.
2. In 12-inch nonstick skillet, heat oil over medium heat until hot but not smoking.
3. Drop 3 tablespoons of the pancake batter into hot oil.
4. With spatula, flatten each pancake against bottom of skillet.
5. Fry 3 to 4 minutes on each side, or until golden brown.
6. Repeat with remaining pancake batter.
7. Drain pancakes on paper towels.

Groats and Swiss Chard

Makes 4 servings.

Swiss chard is a much neglected, delicious winter vegetable. The red variety lends wonderful color to this dish, but if unavailable, green chard is just as tasty.

Oat Bran (g): 17

Calories: 154   Total Fat (g): 8
Cholesterol (mg): 0   Sodium (mg): 361
Sat. Fat (g): 1   Fiber (g): 4

All counts are per serving

---

1 cup oat groats, rinsed and drained
2 tablespoons olive oil
3 garlic cloves, minced
1 bunch red Swiss chard (about 1 pound), washed, trimmed, and chopped (not dried)
2 tablespoons chopped fresh parsley
1 tablespoon fresh lemon juice
1/4 teaspoon salt, or to taste
1/4 teaspoon freshly ground pepper
Grated Parmesan cheese to garnish, optional

1. In medium saucepan over high heat, bring 2 cups water to a boil. Stir in groats; cover, reduce heat and simmer about 45 minutes, until water is absorbed.
2. In 12-inch nonstick skillet, heat oil over medium-high heat; sauté garlic 2 to 3 minutes until lightly browned, stirring frequently.
3. Carefully, add wet chard; cover, reduce heat, and cook 15 to 20 minutes until tender, stirring occasionally.
4. Remove skillet from heat; add parsley, lemon juice, salt, pepper, and cooked groats, stirring to combine. Sprinkle with the cheese, if desired.

Desserts

Chunky Oatmeal Cookies
Makes about 48 cookies.

This is a crisp cookie with a hint of peanut butter.

Oat Bran (g): 8

Calories: 106   Total Fat (g): 6
Cholesterol (mg): 0   Sodium (mg): 50
Sat. Fat (g): 1   Fiber (g): 1

All counts are per serving of two cookies

---

1 cup unsalted margarine	*1½ teaspoons vanilla extract*
One 6-ounce jar chunky peanut butter (½ cup)	*1½ cups all-purpose flour*
	1 teaspoon baking soda
½ cup granulated sugar	*¼ teaspoon salt*
½ cup firmly packed brown sugar	*3 cups rolled oats*
½ cup egg substitute	

1. Preheat oven to 375° F.
2. In large bowl, beat together margarine, peanut butter, and sugars until light and fluffy; beat in egg substitute and vanilla.

3. In medium bowl, combine flour, baking soda, and salt; add to margarine mixture and mix well.
4. Stir in rolled oats; drop by rounded tablespoonsful onto ungreased cookie sheet.
5. Bake 15 minutes until lightly browned; cool on wire rack.
6. Store in tightly covered container.

Raisin-Bread Pudding

Makes 4 servings.

Serve this pudding warm or cold. It is delicious with crushed pineapple or strawberries.

Oat Bran (g): 10	
Calories: 266	Total Fat (g): 4
Cholesterol (mg): 72	Sodium (mg): 276
Sat. Fat (g): 1	Fiber (g): 2.5
All counts are per serving	

6 slices raisin bread, quartered	1/4 cup granulated sugar
1/2 cup oat bran	2 teaspoons vanilla extract
2 cups skim milk	1/4 teaspoon ground cinnamon
1 large egg plus 2 large egg whites, lightly beaten	Pinch of salt

1. Preheat oven to 350° F.; spray a 1 1/2-quart casserole with nonstick cooking spray.
2. Place bread in prepared dish; sprinkle with oat bran and set aside.

3. In medium bowl, whisk together remaining ingredients; pour over bread and oat bran, pressing bread slices down into liquid to saturate. Let stand 10 minutes.
4. Bake, covered, 30 minutes; uncover and bake 30 minutes longer. Let stand 10 minutes.

Streusel Squares

Makes 9 servings.

These squares do a magic trick—they disappear instantly! A once-in-a-while treat.

Oat Bran (g): 6	
Calories: 266	Total Fat (g): 13
Cholesterol (mg): 31	Sodium (mg): 289
Sat. Fat (g): 2	Fiber (g): 1.5
All counts are per serving	

Streusel:
- ½ cup Domino Brownulated light brown sugar
- 2 tablespoons margarine, cut into 8 pieces
- 2 tablespoons oat bran
- ½ teaspoon each ground nutmeg and cinnamon
- ½ cup walnuts, coarsely chopped

Batter:

1 cup all-purpose flour	1 large egg at room
½ cup oat bran	temperature
½ cup Domino	½ cup skim milk
Brownulated light	¼ cup margarine,
brown sugar	melted and cooled
2½ teaspoons baking	1½ teaspoons vanilla
powder	extract
¼ teaspoon salt	

1. Preheat oven to 375° F; spray an 8-inch square baking pan with nonstick cooking spray; set aside.
2. To prepare streusel, in small bowl, combine all ingredients except walnuts, mixing with fingers until crumbly; add walnuts; set aside.
3. To prepare batter, in another bowl, combine flour, oat bran, sugar, baking powder, and salt.
4. In medium bowl, whisk egg until foamy; add remaining ingredients; stir in flour mixture. Mix thoroughly.
5. Pour half the batter into prepared pan, tilting pan to cover bottom; sprinkle ½ cup streusel over batter evenly; pour in remaining batter, spreading it, and top with streusel.
6. Bake 25 to 30 minutes, until wooden toothpick inserted in center comes out clean.
7. Loosen edges with a knife. Cool on rack 10 minutes; remove from pan by placing plate over top and inverting onto rack.

Carrot Cake

Makes 12 servings.

Moist, dense, and delicious.

Oat Bran (g): 8

Calories: 349
Cholesterol (mg): 0
Sat. Fat (g): 2

Total Fat (g): 19
Sodium (mg): 233
Fiber (g): 2.5

All counts are per serving

---

1 cup vegetable oil	½ cup rolled oats
1 cup honey	1 teaspoon baking soda
1 cup egg substitute	1 teaspoon baking
1 teaspoon vanilla	powder
extract	½ teaspoon salt
1¼ cups all-purpose flour	¼ teaspoon each ground
¾ cup oat bran	nutmeg and cinnamon
	3 cups shredded carrots
	(about 6 carrots)

1. Preheat oven to 350° F.; spray a 9-cup tube pan with nonstick cooking spray; set aside.
2. In large bowl of electric mixer, combine oil, honey, egg substitute, and vanilla.
3. In medium bowl, combine remaining ingredients except carrots; gradually add to oil mixture, beating 1 minute.
4. Stir in carrots; pour into prepared pan.
5. Bake 55 to 60 minutes, or until toothpick inserted in center comes out clean.
6. Cool in pan 15 minutes; loosen edges with knife, turn onto rack to cool completely.

Apple Crisp

Makes 8 servings.

This old-fashioned dessert can be enjoyed guilt free. It is extremely high in oat bran and contains only moderate amounts of fat and sugar.

Oat Bran (g): 18

Calories: 253   Total Fat (g): 9
Cholesterol (mg): 0   Sodium (mg): 138
Sat. Fat (g): 2   Fiber (g): 5

All counts are per serving

---

6   *Granny Smith apples (about 2¾ pounds)*
Juice of 1 lemon
1½ cups rolled oats
½ cup oat bran
¼ cup melted margarine
⅓ cup Domino Brownulated light brown sugar

3 tablespoons chopped, slivered almonds
1 teaspoon ground allspice
1 teaspoon vanilla extract
¼ teaspoon salt
½ cup apple juice

1. Preheat oven to 375° F.; spray a 9- x 13-inch baking pan with nonstick cooking spray; set aside.
2. Pare, core, and thinly slice apples; place in pan and drizzle with lemon juice.
3. In medium bowl, combine remaining ingredients except apple juice; spoon onto apples in pan. Pour apple juice evenly over top.
4. Bake 40 to 45 minutes, until crisp.

Blondie Slenders

Makes 18 squares, or 9 servings.

These thin, cake-like squares are light and moist.

```
Oat Bran (g): 8

Calories: 250              Total Fat (g): 10
Cholesterol (mg): 0        Sodium (mg): 307
Sat. Fat (g): 2            Fiber (g): 1.5

All counts are per serving
```

$^2/_3$ cup reduced-calorie tub margarine
1 cup Domino Brownulated light brown sugar
$^3/_4$ cup egg substitute
2 teaspoons vanilla extract

1 cup all-purpose flour
$^1/_2$ cup oat flour
$^1/_2$ cup oat bran
2 teaspoons baking powder
$^1/_4$ teaspoon salt
$^1/_4$ cup mini chocolate chips

1. Preheat oven to 350° F.; spray a jelly-roll pan with nonstick cooking spray; set aside.
2. In medium saucepan, melt margarine over low heat; remove from heat.
3. Add sugar, stirring until combined; add egg substitute and vanilla; continue beating until smooth.
4. In medium bowl, combine flours, oat bran, baking powder, and salt; gradually add liquid ingredients until blended. Fold in chocolate chips.
5. With spatula, spread mixture into prepared pan.
6. Bake 20 to 30 minutes, or until toothpick inserted into center comes out clean.
7. Cool completely in pan on wire rack. Cut into eighteen 2$^1/_2$- x 3$^1/_2$-inch squares.

Caramel Popcorn Balls

Makes 4 servings.

Oats and popcorn—a great combo in this high-fiber treat.

Oat Bran (g): 17

Calories: 314   Total Fat (g): 7
Cholesterol (mg): 0   Sodium (mg): 225
Sat. Fat (g): 1   Fiber (g): 3

All counts are per serving

---

*¹/₂ cup firmly packed dark
   brown sugar*
¹/₄ cup light corn syrup
2 tablespoons margarine

¹/₄ teaspoon salt
4 cups popped popcorn
1 cup rolled oats

1. In Dutch oven, over medium-high heat, combine sugar, corn syrup, margarine, and salt; cook 2 minutes, until sugar is melted, stirring constantly.
2. Remove from heat; stir in popcorn and oats until coated.
3. Dip hands into cold water; shape mixture into 8 balls about 2 inches in diameter. Place on wax paper; cool completely.
4. Wrap individually in plastic wrap.

Gingered Pear Cobbler

Makes 4 servings.

One of the most healthful desserts you can make—high in oat bran and low in saturated fat!

Oat Bran (g): 17

Calories: 340   Total Fat (g): 7
Cholesterol (mg): < 1   Sodium (mg): 323
Sat. Fat (g): < 1   Fiber (g): 3

All counts are per serving

3/4 cup plus 1 tablespoon   1/8 teaspoon salt
     oat bran   2   tablespoons
1/2 cup all-purpose flour   margarine, cut into
2   tablespoons   small pieces
     granulated sugar   1/2 cup skim milk
1 1/2 teaspoons baking   Two 16-ounce cans pear
     powder   halves in light syrup,
1/4 teaspoon ground   reserving 1/2 cup juice
     cinnamon   1/4 teaspoon ground
                                    ginger

1. Preheat oven to 400° F.
2. In medium bowl, combine the 3/4 cup oat bran, flour, sugar, baking powder, cinnamon, and salt. Cut margarine into mixture until it resembles fine crumbs. Stir in milk until batter forms.
3. Arrange pears in 8-inch square baking pan. In cup, combine reserved juice, the 1 tablespoon oat bran, and ginger, and pour over pears.
4. Drop batter by heaping tablespoonfuls onto pears.
5. Bake 25 to 30 minutes, until lightly browned and toothpick inserted in center of pastry comes out clean.

Burnt Almond Gelato

Makes 4 servings.

Although this is an ice milk, it's reminiscent of Italian gelato, lighter than ice cream—a delicious guilt-free treat anytime.

Oat Bran (g): 13

Calories: 254   Total Fat (g): 5
Cholesterol (mg): 6   Sodium (mg): 130
Sat. Fat (g): 1   Fiber (g): 2

All counts are per serving

One 12-ounce can   ½ teaspoon almond
    evaporated skim milk   extract
1   cup lowfat (1%) milk   ¾ cup rolled oats
⅓   cup granulated sugar   ¼ cup sliced almonds
1   teaspoon vanilla
    extract

1. To prepare gelato, in 4-cup measure, combine evaporated and lowfat milk, sugar, and extracts; place in container of ice-cream machine and process, following manufacturer's instructions.
2. In medium skillet, over medium heat, toast oats and almonds 5 to 7 minutes, stirring frequently.
3. Cool oat mixture; stir into gelato.
4. To store, spoon gelato into freezer container with lid, pressing wax paper onto surface of gelato. Cover tightly.
5. To serve, remove from freezer; let soften 30 minutes or until "scoopable."

In medium bowl, combine eggs, oil, remaining 1
cup water, and yeast mixture; pour into well.
Stir mixture with wooden spoon until well combined.
and ball forms.

Baked Goods

Braided Oat Bread
Makes 16 servings.

This is a dense bread—great with soup!

Oat Bran (g): 10	
Calories: 169	Total Fat (g): 4
Cholesterol (mg): 34	Sodium (mg): 286
Sat. Fat (g): < 1	Fiber (g): 2
All counts are per serving	

1¼ cups warm water
   (105°–115° F.)
1 package active dry
   yeast
2 teaspoons granulated
   sugar
3¾ cups all-purpose flour
1½ cups oat bran

2 teaspoons salt
2 large eggs at room
   temperature
2 tablespoons vegetable
   oil
½ large egg white
1 tablespoon poppy seeds

1. In cup, combine ¼ cup of the warm water, yeast,
   and sugar; let stand 10 minutes.
2. In large bowl, combine 3 cups of the flour, oat bran,
   and salt; make a well in center.
3. In medium bowl, combine eggs, oil, remaining 1
   cup water, and yeast mixture; pour into well.

3. In medium bowl, combine eggs, oil, remaining 1 cup water, and yeast mixture; pour into well.

4. Stir mixture with wooden spoon until well combined and ball forms.

5. Turn dough onto floured surface; knead, gradually adding remaining 3/4 cup flour, about 10 minutes, until dough is smooth and elastic.

6. Place dough in large bowl, sprayed with nonstick cooking spray, turning to coat top surface. Cover tightly with plastic wrap; let rise in warm, draft-free place until doubled in size, about 1 1/2 hours.

7. Punch down dough; divide in 3 equal parts; with hands, roll each part to 16-inch length, tapered at end.

8. Place parallel on jelly-roll pan sprayed with nonstick cooking spray.

9. Braid ropes starting at center and working to ends; press each end firmly and tuck under. Brush with egg white; sprinkle with poppy seeds. Cover lightly with foil; let rise in warm, draft-free place until doubled in size, about 30 minutes.

10. Preheat oven to 375° F. Remove foil and bake 45–55 minutes, or until sounds hollow when tapped on bottom.

Jalapeño Cornbread

Makes 6 servings.

A classic chili sidekick.

Oat Bran (g): 7

Calories: 244   Total Fat (g): 10
Cholesterol (mg): 46   Sodium (mg): 447
Sat. Fat (g): 2   Fiber (g): 2

All counts are per serving

---

1   cup all-purpose flour   ½ small jalapeño pepper,
½ cup corn meal   seeded and finely
½ cup oat bran   chopped
2   teaspoons baking   1   cup skim milk
    powder   ¼ cup margarine, melted
1   teaspoon granulated   and cooled
    sugar   1   large egg, lightly
½ teaspoon salt   beaten

1. Preheat oven to 400° F.; spray an 8-inch square pan
   with nonstick cooking spray; set aside.
2. In large bowl, combine dry ingredients and jalapeño
   pepper; stir in liquid ingredients; pour into prepared
   pan.
3. Bake 25 to 30 minutes, or until toothpick inserted in
   center comes out clean.
4. Cool on rack 10 minutes.

Pecan-Bran-Date Bread
Makes 1 loaf, 12 servings.

This molasses-flavored bread is moist and rich.

Oat Bran (g): 7

Calories: 186   Total Fat (g): 4
Cholesterol (mg): 23   Sodium (mg): 112
Sat. Fat (g): < 1   Fiber (g): 2.5

All counts are per serving

---

1 cup orange juice	1 1/4 cups all-purpose flour
1 cup chopped pitted dates	1 cup oat bran
1 large egg at room temperature	1 teaspoon baking powder
1/3 cup molasses	1 teaspoon baking soda
1 teaspoon vanilla extract	1/2 cup coarsely chopped pecans
	Pinch of salt, optional

1. Preheat oven to 350° F.; spray a 5- x 9-inch loaf pan with nonstick cooking spray; set aside.
2. In small saucepan, over high heat, bring orange juice to a boil; add dates and remove from heat; set aside.
3. In small bowl, beat egg until frothy; add molasses and vanilla, mix well.
4. In large bowl, combine flour, oat bran, baking powder, and baking soda; add nuts and dates with orange juice.
5. Stir in egg/molasses mixture until just combined.
6. Pour into prepared pan. Spread top evenly; bake 45 to 50 minutes, or until toothpick inserted in center comes out clean.
7. Cool on rack in pan 10 minutes; remove from pan and turn onto rack to cool completely.

Jumbo Onion-Dill Popovers

Makes 4 large popovers.

For a great summer lunch, serve these with grilled vegetables, or a cold soup.

Oat Bran (g): 5

Calories: 119   Total Fat (g): 2
Cholesterol (mg): 69   Sodium (mg): 194
Sat. Fat (g): <1   Fiber (g): 1

All counts are per serving

½ cup all-purpose flour
¼ cup oat bran
¼ teaspoon salt
*1 tablespoon dried
minced onion*
¼ teaspoon dried dillweed

*⅛ teaspoon freshly
ground black pepper*
½ cup skim milk
*1 large egg plus 2 large
egg whites at room
temperature, lightly
beaten*

1. Preheat oven to 450° F.; spray four 3½-inch muffin
   cups* with nonstick cooking spray; heat in oven 5
   minutes before filling cups.
2. In large bowl, sift together flour, oat bran, and salt;
   add minced onion, dill, and pepper and combine.
3. Whisk in milk, egg, and egg whites.
4. Fill each warmed muffin cup halfway with batter; bake
   15 minutes.
5. Reduce oven temperature to 350° F. Bake 15 minutes
   longer, until popovers are puffed and browned.
6. Prick each popover to let steam escape; bake 5 minutes longer.

*If using popover pan with cups 2¼ inches in diameter, this recipe
will make 8 popovers.

Colossal Cranberry Muffins
Makes 6 large muffins.

For cranberry lovers! A fun brunch muffin.

Oat Bran (g): 16

Calories: 294   Total Fat (g): 11
Cholesterol (mg): 1   Sodium (mg): 228
Sat. Fat (g): 1   Fiber (g): 4

All counts are per serving

3/4 cup oat bran
3/4 cup all-purpose flour
1/2 cup rolled oats
1/2 cup Domino Brownulated light brown sugar
2 tablespoons granulated sugar
1 teaspoon baking powder
1/2 teaspoon baking soda
1/2 teaspoon salt
1/2 teaspoon dried orange peel
1 cup cranberries
2/3 cup buttermilk
3 tablespoons vegetable oil
1/4 cup egg substitute
1/2 teaspoon vanilla extract

1. Preheat oven to 400° F.; spray 6 jumbo (3½ inches in diameter) muffin cups with nonstick cooking spray. Can also be done in regular size muffin cups (makes 12).
2. In large bowl, combine dry ingredients, including peel; add cranberries.
3. Pour in liquid ingredients; mix with a fork, but do not overbeat.
4. Fill prepared muffin cups with equal amounts of mixture.
5. For jumbo muffins bake 25 minutes, and for regular muffins bake 15 to 20 minutes, or until toothpick inserted in center comes out clean.
6. Let cool in pan 10 minutes; loosen edges with a knife, turn onto rack to cool completely.

Puffed "Pita" Sandwich Rolls

Makes 8 rolls.

Tasty even without a filling. These are thicker than pita bread and slice like a roll.

```
                    Oat Bran (g): 10

    Calories: 265              Total Fat (g): 9
    Cholesterol (mg): 35       Sodium (mg): 151
    Sat. Fat (g): 1            Fiber (g): 4.5

    All counts are per serving
```

1½ cups all-purpose flour
1   cup whole wheat flour
1   cup oat bran
1   package quick-acting
    active dry yeast
2   tablespoons
    granulated sugar
½   teaspoon salt

½ cup warm water (120°–130° F.)
¼ cup warm milk (120°–130° F.)
¼ cup vegetable oil (120°–130° F.)
1 large egg at room temperature, lightly beaten

1. In large bowl of electric mixer, on low speed, combine 1 cup of the all-purpose flour, the whole wheat flour, oat bran, yeast, sugar, and salt.
2. Add remaining liquid ingredients, including egg; beat on low speed, scraping bowl frequently, about 1 minute. Stir in enough remaining flour to make dough easy to handle.
3. Turn dough on lightly floured surface; knead until smooth and elastic, about 5 minutes, adding more flour if necessary. Cover dough, let rest 10 minutes.
4. Spray 2 baking sheets with nonstick cooking spray.

5. Divide dough into 8 equal pieces. Shape each piece into a ball, then flatten each and spread with fingers into a 4-inch circle.
6. Place dough circles on prepared sheets. Cover; let rise in warm, draft-free place until doubled in size (about 1 hour).
7. Preheat oven to 400° F. Bake 12 to 18 minutes until lightly browned and the rolls sound hollow when tapped on bottom. Turn onto rack to cool.
8. Slice rolls crosswise with serrated knife to serve. Store in sealable plastic bag. May be frozen.

Cardamom-Lemon Biscuits

Makes 8 biscuits.

Cardamom, an aromatic spice, adds an unusual flavor to these quick biscuits.

Oat Bran (g): 8

Calories: 125
Cholesterol (mg): < 1
Sat. Fat (g): < 1

Total Fat (g): 3
Sodium (mg): 273
Fiber (g): 1.5

All counts are per serving

1½ cups Bisquick
¾ cup oat bran
1 teaspoon grated lemon peel

½ teaspoon ground cardamom
⅔ cup skim milk

1. Preheat oven to 450° F.
2. In medium bowl, combine dry ingredients; stir in milk and mix until combined.
3. Drop by spoonfuls on ungreased baking sheet; bake 12 to 15 minutes, or until toothpick inserted in center comes out clean.

Parmesan-Black Olive Bread
Makes 1 loaf, or 16 servings.

This olive-flecked loaf is not only a great dinner bread when thinly sliced, it's also perfect for cocktails!

Oat Bran (g): 9

Calories: 141
Cholesterol (mg): 4
Sat. Fat (g): 1

Total Fat (g): 5
Sodium (mg): 195
Fiber (g): 2

All counts are per serving

---

1   package active dry
    yeast
1   teaspoon granulated
    sugar
1¼ cups warm water
    (105°–115° F.)
2   cups all-purpose flour
1¾ cups oat bran

1   cup grated Parmesan
    cheese, reserving 2
    tablespoons
½   teaspoon salt
2   tablespoons olive oil
½   cup sliced pitted black
    olives
½   large egg white

1. Spray large mixing bowl with nonstick cooking spray; set aside. In small bowl, combine yeast, sugar, and ¾ cup of the warm water; let stand 10 minutes.
2. In food processor fitted with steel blade, combine 1½ cups of the flour, the oat bran, cheese, salt, and oil; with machine running add remaining ½ cup warm water and yeast mixture. Add up to remaining ½ cup flour, a little at a time, pulsing until ball forms. Add flour as needed. Discard any unused flour.
3. Place dough in prepared bowl, turning to coat; cover with plastic wrap and let rise in warm, draft-free place until tripled in size, about 1½ to 2 hours.
4. Punch dough down; turn onto lightly floured surface, sprinkled with reserved 2 tablespoons of cheese. Knead in olives.

5. Shape dough into 16-inch loaf, tapered at ends, place on baking sheet. Cover with a towel and let rise in warm, draft-free place until doubled in size, about 1½ to 2 hours.
6. Preheat oven to 425° F.
7. Brush loaf with egg white; bake about 25 minutes, or until golden and loaf sounds hollow when tapped on bottom.
8. Turn bread onto rack to cool.

Tiny Tofu Teacakes
Makes 12 teacakes, or 4 servings.

Fill a basket with these tiny taste treats; add Buttermilk Currant Scones (p. 106), and sit down for a relaxing afternoon tea.

Oat Bran (g): 7

Calories: 211   Total Fat (g): 9
Cholesterol (mg): 68   Sodium (mg): 280
Sat. Fat (g): 9   Fiber (g): 1.5

All counts are per serving

⅓ cup all-purpose flour	1 cup mashed drained tofu
⅓ cup oat bran	3 tablespoons honey
1½ teaspoons baking powder	2 tablespoons margarine, melted and cooled
Pinch of salt	1 large egg at room temperature

1. Preheat oven to 400° F.; spray 12 mini muffin pan cups with nonstick cooking spray, set aside.
2. In medium bowl, combine flour, oat bran, baking powder, and salt.

3. In blender, purée remaining ingredients until smooth; add to flour mixture; combine with fork until just blended. Divide evenly among muffin cups.
4. Bake 20 to 25 minutes, or until toothpick inserted comes out clean. Cool on rack 10 minutes.

Buttermilk-Currant Scones

Makes 20 small scones, or 10 servings.

Very oaty in flavor. Terrific with preserves and marmalades.

Oat Bran (g): 8

Calories: 66   Total Fat (g): 2
Cholesterol (mg): < 1   Sodium (mg): 74
Sat. Fat (g): < 1   Fiber (g): 1

All counts are per 2 scone serving

---

1   cup all-purpose flour
½ cup oat bran
½ cup rolled oats or steel-cut oats
1   tablespoon granulated sugar
1   teaspoon baking powder
½ teaspoon baking soda
3   tablespoons chilled margarine, cut in pieces
¼ cup currants
¾ cup buttermilk
1   large egg white

1. Preheat oven to 400° F.; spray baking sheet with non-stick cooking spray; set aside.
2. In large bowl, combine all dry ingredients; cut in margarine until mixture is crumbly. Stir in currants.
3. Add buttermilk; combine to form dough.
4. Turn dough onto lightly floured surface; knead lightly 10 times; sprinkle lightly with flour if sticky. Roll to

1/2-inch thickness; cut with floured 2-inch round biscuit cutter using all dough.
5. Place scones on prepared baking sheet; brush with egg white. Bake 10 to 12 minutes, or until golden.
6. Turn onto rack to cool.

"Buttery" Brioche

Makes 2 loaves (sixteen 1/2 inch slices per loaf).

This is a very light bread, similar to French brioche, minus the saturated fat.

Oat Bran per slice (g): 3

Calories: 192   Total Fat (g): 7
Cholesterol (mg): 17   Sodium (mg): 221
Sat. Fat (g): 2   Fiber (g): 2

All counts are per serving

---

3   cups all-purpose flour   1 package active dry yeast
1 1/2 cups oat flour   1 large egg plus 1 large
1   cup skim milk   egg white at room
1/2 cup margarine   temperature, lightly
2   tablespoons   beaten
     granulated sugar   2 teaspoons salt
2   teaspoons butter
     extract

1. In a bowl, combine flours; set aside.
2. In medium saucepan, over medium-high heat, combine milk, margarine, sugar, and butter extract; bring to a boil, stirring frequently.

3. Remove from heat; pour into large bowl and cool to lukewarm (105°–115° F.).

4. Stir in yeast; let stand 10 minutes.

5. Add egg and egg white and salt; whisk in 3 to 3½ cups of the flour mixture, 1 cup at a time, until dough forms.

6. Turn dough out onto lightly floured surface; knead about 10 minutes, adding remaining flour mixture until dough is elastic and smooth.

7. Place dough in large bowl, sprayed with nonstick cooking spray; turn dough to coat top.

8. Cover with plastic wrap; place in warm, draft-free place until tripled in size, about 2 hours.

9. Spray two 8- x 3¾- x 2½-inch aluminum loaf pans with nonstick cooking spray.

10. Punch the dough down; divide into 2 equal pieces. Shape each piece into a loaf to fit pan. Place in prepared pan; cover with plastic wrap; let rise again until doubled in size, about 1 hour.

11. Preheat oven to 375° F.; bake 30 to 40 minutes, or until golden and sounds hollow when tapped on bottom.

12. Cool on rack in pans 10 minutes; remove and cool completely.

Drinks and Shakes

Chocolate Tofu Shake

Makes 1 serving.

An eye-opener complete with protein and calcium. For a healthful breakfast on the go add a muffin.

Oat Bran (g): 8

Calories: 199   Total Fat (g): 5
Cholesterol (mg): 6   Sodium (mg): 120
Sat. Fat (g): 1   Fiber (g): 2

All counts are per serving

½ cup skim milk   *1½ tablespoons oat bran*
¼ cup cubed, drained   2 *teaspoons chocolate*
tofu   *syrup*
¼ cup lowfat yogurt   1 *teaspoon granulated*
                                sugar

Place all ingredients in blender; blend until smooth.

Strawberry/Banana Perk-Up

Makes 1 serving.

A terrific afternoon pick-me-up.

Oat Bran (g): 8

Calories: 244   Total Fat (g): 3
Cholesterol (mg): 7   Sodium (mg): 195
Sat. Fat (g): 1   Fiber (g): 4

All counts are per serving

---

³/₄ cup buttermilk   *¹/₂ ripe banana, sliced*
¹/₂ cup strawberries,   *1¹/₂ tablespoons oat bran*
*   quartered**   *1   tablespoon honey*

Place all ingredients in blender; blend until smooth. Pour into 12-ounce glass.

*Frozen strawberries may be used.

Ice Milk Malted

Makes 1 serving.

The malted milk powder makes this smoothie taste as good as the soda shop's!

Oat Bran (g): 8	
Calories: 224	Total Fat (g): 5
Cholesterol (mg): 14	Sodium (mg): 225
Sat. Fat (g): 2	Fiber (g): 1
All counts are per serving	

½   cup skim milk
1½ tablespoons oat bran

1   tablespoon malted milk
     powder
½ cup vanilla ice milk

1. Place all ingredients except ice milk in blender; blend until combined.
2. Add ice milk; blend only until mixed.

Index

About the Author

Linda Romanelli Leahy is a professional recipe developer and food and wine consultant. As test kitchen director and associate food editor at WEIGHT WATCHERS MAGAZINE she developed and tested virtually all of the recipes published over a two-year period (ending November 1988)—more than 600 recipes in all! She resides in Brooklyn, New York, with her husband and two children.

EAT WELL...
LIVE WELL